100 Ways to Teach Language Online

Powerful Tools for the Online and Flipped Classroom Language Teacher

Shane Dixon, Justin Shewell, and Jenny Crandell

WAYZGOOSE PRESS

ISBN-13: 978-1-938757-77-8

Edited by Dorothy E. Zemach. Book design by DJ Rogers.
Published in the United States by Wayzgoose Press.

Table of Contents

Note: Activities are sometimes accompanied by a printable and photocopiable template.

A printable template is indicated when you see this icon next to the activity: pg. 00

How to Use This Book

The activities here were selected based on several criteria. The first is that the activity must, above all, be academically sound. Thus, these activities all have roots, although sometimes contested, in research-based concepts. The second important characteristic is that they be, on the whole, easy for you to follow and implement. These activities were chosen because they can be easily adapted to a number of contexts, and they take little to no time to prepare. A final feature is that each and every activity should be level agnostic, meaning that it shouldn't matter if your learners are beginners or advanced.

As you read the following activities, keep in mind the following suggestions:

- Review all 100 tips again and again. This manual is often best used when you feel "stuck" or unable to think of how best to teach a particular subject matter. In other words, think of this book as a way to jumpstart your brain...especially when it stalls.
- Use the table of contents. The table of contents provides the titles for all of the tips to quickly remind you of areas of interest as well as specific activities.
- Pay it forward. Feel free to share your favorite activities on social media, get our newsletter at http://language-warriors.com, and join our language warriors group on Facebook at: https://www.facebook.com/groups/LanguageWarrior/

Introduction

Good teaching is good teaching. Whether you are engaging learners in a traditional brick-and-mortar classroom, in a flipped or hybrid classroom, or find yourself completely online, some things never change. Organization, dynamism, a sense of humor, an ability to break things down...these are hallmarks of instruction at any level and in any context. If you are a good teacher in one arena, you will likely be a good teacher in another.

That stated, the online world presents a particular challenge for traditional teachers, especially those who have yet to make the switch to a digital classroom environment. Traditional chalkboards, group and pair work, paper worksheets, and handouts are being replaced with digital whiteboards, chatrooms, discussion boards, and online quizzes and flashcards.

Besides a change in tools is a shift in learners. The modern online learner tends to be more autonomous, have more digital literacy (often more than the teacher), and have specific outcomes in mind. Many of our online students ask us to engage them in specific vocabulary suited to a job or hobby. Thus, online teachers often shift their focus to include specific needs and desires of the learner, making the teacher not only an instructor but something of a guide or consultant as well.

One useful way to think about the shift from a traditional classroom to an online classroom is to imagine a painter having to give up painting entirely in order to pursue sculpting. While both can express the same theme and content, there is a different set of tools that can and should be exploited. In other words, you are still creating art, and you can still have many of the same themes and ideas, but you must use a different set of tools.

A Different Set of Tools

This book is your toolbox. It is intended to provide you activities to help you make the switch, metaphorically, from painting to sculpting. You'll discover that while there are many activities that can be modified to suit any context, there are some activities that are different precisely because of the change in medium or learner. You'll also notice that even familiar activities will need careful adjustment in order to work in the online world, and while we attempt to do some of that work here, keep in mind that your job will be to continue to modify any suggested activity to the real needs and concerns of your learners.

Get Visual

OIn the online world, being able to project pictures, videos, or activities on the screen is particularly helpful. There are many software programs or apps available to do this, and checking with fellow online teachers and search engines should reveal many possibilities. What are you looking for when you want to "get visual"? You will often want to share your screen with students (as opposed to holding up a picture, prop, or your phone) instead of holding an object in your hand.

Having slide presentations is an extremely effective tool for visually displaying content. With just your voice and a slide presentation, you can often share entire lessons. Slide presentations help you get visual with vocabulary words because you can add pictures to illustrate the word. The same is true for question prompts, tricky descriptions, and so forth. Adding video clips into your presentation can give added interest as well.

Think Ecosystem

When training online language learners, one concept to keep in mind is that of a language ecosystem. This refers to the system that most successful language learners use, whether consciously or not. The ecosystem concept is based on knowledge gained from the good language learner studies of the 1980's and 1990's (for a brief overview, see Ellis, 2008). Of the many salient findings, it was discovered that successful language learners were able to master a language better and faster because of their ability to extend classroom practice outward. Good language learners understood this simple truth:

In determining language success, what learners do OUTSIDE the classroom has much more impact than what happens INSIDE.

Thus, it is important for you not only to teach learners within a classroom setting (online or otherwise), but to help your learners extend their language experience to the greater world beyond your classroom. This can be done by creating incentives and rewards for those who engage in outside material. For example, many teachers invite students to bring such materials into their lessons. You might ask students to bring a favorite song, story, or poem in the target language.

Another ecosystem activity involves the formation of reading and listening goals. In order to incentivize students to read outside the online classroom, for example, you might create a reading challenge (This week's challenge is to read 50 pages!) and have students log their progress.

One final example is the formation of conversation groups. You can do this in several ways. For example, you might form "after class" reading circles, conversation clubs, or movie nights (and yes, all of these can be done online!). In keeping in line with the goal of learner autonomy, however, it might be better still to train learners how to find and engage with conversation partners on their own.

In short, while a language ecosystem means that a learner must take control of his or her own language learning, the teacher's role is still significant. A teacher, and the school that the teacher attends, can and should incentivize students to participate in the world outside of the classroom. Properly defined, we suggest that the ecosystem model of language learning, from the point of view of the teacher, describes a holistic environment that encourages and extends the learning and application of the language beyond the classroom through a diverse system of activities and incentives. Metaphorically speaking, while the learner, in this conceptualization, takes on the role of adventurer, the teacher becomes the guide.

Here is a visual representation of the ecosystem model, attending to the features already discussed, but from the point of view of the learner.

Ecosystem Model of Language Learning

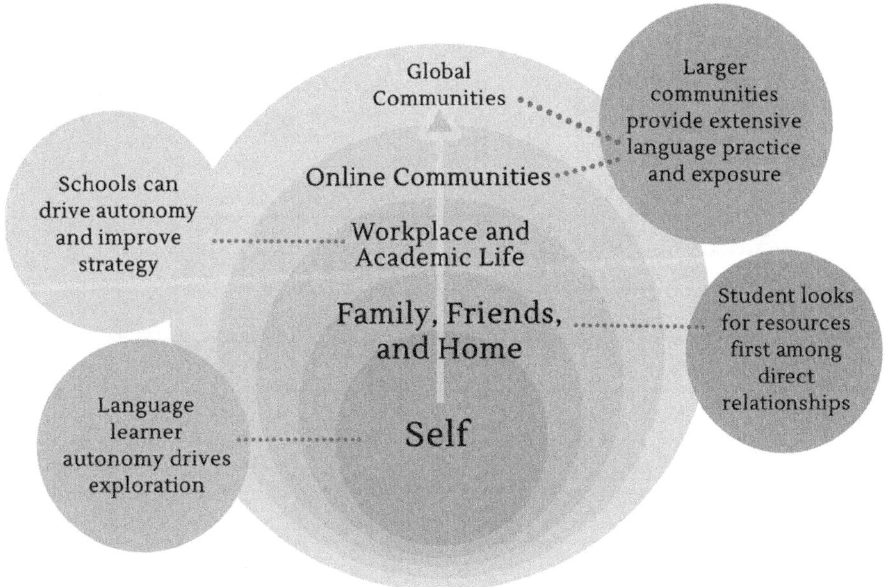

Dixon and Shewell, 2020

In this graphic, you'll see that success for language learning rests primarily with the learner him or herself (Self). The term language learner autonomy implies that to successfully learn a language, one must look beyond the classroom and toward a variety of resources including books, movies, apps, classroom instruction, and so forth. This approach promotes exploration, introspection, balancing objectives, risk taking, and friendship.

Within this framework of autonomy, a learner is immersed in a number of communities (from more familiar to less familiar), represented by a series of concentric circles. Since there is a direct correlation between language success and a learner's use of the language with close relationships (Dixon 2001), family, friends, and homelife are preferred when a learner explores language materials and partners. This is followed by the finding of resources among teachers and fellow students in academic life, and then, beyond that, to online and global communities.

Dixon, S. (2001) A sociolinguistic study of ESL students at Brigham Young University. Retrieved from ProQuest.

Ellis, R. (2008). The study of second language acquisition. Oxford: Oxford University Press.

Lesson Planning Overview

Instructional design varies from discipline to discipline, and there are many models that might evoke a similar look to lesson planning. Nonetheless, whether you are teaching face to face, online, or perhaps in a hybrid/flipped classroom model (both online and in person), most lesson planning includes the basic elements shown here.

The terms used here are somewhat universal, but other terms exist and, once again, vary from context to context. For example, the term warm up is sometimes referred to as a theme introduction or an attention getter, or as a process of activating/engaging learners. For a deeper look at lesson planning elements, we recommend considering a serious look at the ECRIF model (Kurzweil & Scholl, 2007) or Bloom's taxonomy (we recommend looking at the revised taxonomy by Anderson & Krathwohl, 2001).

Common Elements of Lesson Planning
Warm Up
Objective Discussion
Present and Model
Guided or Controlled Practice
Less Guided or Controlled Practice
Independent Practice
Assessment

Step #1: Warm up or Prepare Students – In this portion of a lesson, you warm up the students by activating their background knowledge and introducing new knowledge. You may do this by presenting some key vocabulary, eliciting their knowledge of the subject, using prediction exercises, etc.

Step #2: Discuss the Objectives – In this portion of a lesson, you attempt to give learners a metacognitive understanding of the lesson itself. In simpler terms, you—either explicitly or implicitly—are trying to help students learn WHY they are doing what they are doing, and HOW these objectives, if obtained, might help them. Teachers who engage in these kinds of metacognitive strategies tend to have much more highly motivated students. You will also attain better clarity and focus by having the objectives clearly stated and understood.

Step #3: Present Instruction/Model – In this portion of the lesson, you give students new information they must know or new skills that they must acquire. Here you attempt to scaffold, explain, or otherwise break down information for students to grasp the new concepts. In addition to presenting or instructing, you are encouraged to provide models (examples) for students to follow. For example, you might give a sample dialogue, a model essay, or put the necessary vocabulary to be acquired in example sentences.

Step #4: Guided or Controlled Practice (Practice #1) – In this portion of a lesson, students are invited to practice their new skills and become familiar and comfortable with them. For difficult language concepts, this practice is often very controlled, meaning that it is done with a lot of guidance from either you or other expert helpers.

Step #5: Less-guided Practice (Practice #2) – Following a controlled practice, students are often given practice that has fewer constraints and higher difficulty. For example, rather than doing an activity with you, students might do an activity in pairs or groups. In addition, the activity itself might be modified to provide greater learner autonomy. However, you still facilitate learning by answering questions and providing support to the groups or pairs, and the activity itself should help students to gain more comfort with the language required.

Step #6: Independent Practice (Practice #3) – After a sufficient amount of pair or group work, the students are given an independent activity. This often means that the student will work alone to demonstrate the knowledge or skill that they have acquired. This can be done through a quiz or testing scenario, or some sort of performance such as a presentation or written representation of their newly acquired language skills.

Step #7: Assessment – Evaluating student work can happen at any stage of a lesson. **Formative** assessment generally refers to the kind of assessment that is done during instruction, and could include asking questions, giving informal quizzes, and eliciting student participation. **Summative** assessment, such as a quiz, test, or evaluation, often follows an independent practice, and is meant to measure a student's ability to attain the objectives set out in the lesson plan. It is meant not only as a measure of the students, but can also provide feedback to you as to how well the instruction was received, and what parts of the instruction need continued support.

A lesson plan template is provided that includes these basic steps. Please note that this lesson plan template represents a theoretical construct only, and should not be used in a lockstep manner. In other words, novice teachers might be tempted to provide three practices (controlled, less-controlled, and independent) for every lesson plan, but this would be a mistake. Some language concepts require many MORE than three practices to attain fluency, and some language concepts might be acquired without any practice at all. Thus, you would be wise to gauge the amount of instruction and practice needed, and modify accordingly. Since this template is subject to a kind of reductionist abuse, it is highly recommended that you use it with the recognition that any and all of these steps can be skipped or put in a different order.

Kurzweil, J., & Scholl, M. (2007). School for international training frameworks for language teaching: understanding teaching through learning. New York: McGraw-Hill.

Anderson, L. W., & Krathwohl, D. R. (2001). A Taxonomy for learning, teaching, and assessing: a revision of Bloom's taxonomy of educational objectives. New York: Longman.

Lesson Plan

Business/Materials	Lesson Objectives

Review/Warm Up

Instruct and Model	R	W	L	S

Guided Practice	R	W	L	S

Independent Practice	R	W	L	S

Assessment	R	W	L	S

Part I: The Top Ten Most Common Activities in the Digital Universe

Before we discuss specific activities, let's review some of the fundamental aspects of good online language instruction.

First, there is an audiovisual aspect to online learning that is crucial. Your ability to toggle between pictures, for example, or write clearly on a digital whiteboard, is key. Many of these skills you can improve with practice, but you should note that a good online teacher truly has a command of audio/visual tools to make the experience more rewarding.

Second, you'll want to avoid the talking head syndrome. While a lecture in a classroom can sometimes last an entire hour, the online world requires a more interactive style. In fact, if you create a video for online use, the standard within the field is to keep that video to about 4-6 minutes long. Any longer and students begin to tune out! Even in traditional university classes where long lectures are often permissible, good instructional design is likely not achieved when a teacher simply speaks for an hour. This "talking head" syndrome is symptomatic of a lot of poorly designed university courses that make their way into an online format.

Dr. Richard Mayer identifies 12 Principles of Multimedia that are worth considering. While we won't review them all here, you should note that we have found that many of the principles become clear when you think of yourself in the roll of a director rather than a classroom teacher A keen eye toward the visual (invest in a quality webcam; pay attention to good lighting) and excellent audio quality (get a good microphone!) is essential.

Also important to the process is the need to consider the amount of work done AWAY from your instruction, meaning that much of your work as an online teacher is to create tasks for students to do after the face-to-face session you hold with them. While there are a number of tools to help you do this, we present you with some of the most common activities to help you "flip" the classroom, meaning that students will have assignments outside of your designated "class" time.

1. INFORMATION GAP

In the online world, often you will invite learners to work with each other. But how do you get two learners, who often do not speak English well, to converse? One answer is to use an information gap. Information gap refers to an activity where a learner is given an incomplete set of information, and must interact with another learner to obtain that information. In other words, the point of an information gap activity is to invite learners to collaborate with each other to fill in missing information.

This is most commonly done online by providing alternate information in the form of worksheets (Worksheets A and B). Students will work in pairs (Student A has Worksheet A; Student B has worksheet B). In pairs, students ask each other questions in order to fill out their worksheet.

For example, a worksheet could be "10 Facts About Airplanes." Worksheet A would have 5 facts, and Worksheet B would have another 5 facts. Students have to ask each other questions to get all 10 facts.

Worksheets can have clues to help students form questions. Often students can use the phrase *I don't know*... to ask questions.

Example 1
Student A: I don't know when the first airplane was invented.
Student B: It was in 1903. I don't know who made the first successful airplane.
Student A: Wilbur and Orville Wright made the first successful airplane.

Or they might ask questions directly (especially after a lesson on question formation):

Example 2
Student A: How many airplanes are flying in the world?
Student B: About 10,000 airplanes are flying right now. How many airlines are there in

the world?
Student A: There are more than 5,000 airlines in the world.

Information Gap Creators:

1. https://quickworksheets.net/worksheet-generators/information-gap/about
2. https://www.johnsesl.com/generators/gapfill/gapfill.shtml
3. http://random-idea-english.blogspot.com/2012/06/teacher-tools-information-gap-generator.html

2. CLOZE PASSAGE EXERCISE pg. 75

The word *cloze* is jargon meaning "fill in the blank" or "missing information." A cloze passage generally has missing words or phrases in the form of a space (Example: *George Washington purportedly stated that he never told a* ____). Students listen to an audio passage, either recorded or spoken, and fill in the blank with the missing information. The cloze passage is a popular language activity because it gives students an opportunity to listen to a song, conversation, or topic that uses authentic language.

In online environments, it is common to use cloze passage generators (even a multiple choice quiz creator will work) to see if students can understand a song or passage. Some cloze passage generators will remove the words of the passage for you, although most will allow you to remove the words yourself. Most will also allow you the option of creating a word bank (which makes it easier for students).

Generally, when conducting a cloze passage listening exercise, students will listen to the passage at least twice (the first time to solve, and a second time to confirm their answers).

While this activity is often done during the online instruction, students in upper levels can be given cloze passages for homework, and some students even create cloze passages themselves. For example, you might invite a learner to share a favorite song with you or a fellow classmate.

Cloze Passage Generators:

1. https://www.subjectcoach.com/englishworksheetgenerator/clozetestworksheetmaker
2. https://www.controlaltachieve.com/2017/04/create-cloze-tests.html
3. https://quickworksheets.net/worksheet-generators/cloze-test/about
4. https://www.edhelper.com/cloze.htm

3. ONLINE JOURNALS

Blogs and online journals are certainly not new. However, using them to detail language learning is. An online journal is one of the best kinds of language learning because instead of reciting memorized curriculum, it allows learners to express their own opinions, daily habits, lifestyle, tastes and preferences, and so forth. Journals are particularly successful at helping students open up to language as a real opportunity to share ideas, engage in critical thinking, or demonstrate a particular language function (For example, if you wanted learners to use the past tense, you could use the prompt, *Write about a past experience that...).*

Assigning an online learner a weekly journal article can be a wonderful way to engage in the learner's life and interests. Furthermore, it can encourage other learners in the class to share and learn about each other as well. You may wish to use journals as a way of measuring language output, and can tailor your lessons when you notice incorrect grammatical forms. You may also wish to start a class with an online learner by reviewing the online journal entry and by making suggestions, comments, and compliments.
Note: some learners may not wish for a language learning blog or journal to be made public, so make sure to help the learner set proper sharing and privacy settings.

Places to Create a Blog or Online Journal:

1. https://bytelyfe.app
2. https://penzu.com/
3. https://www.wix.com/
4. https://www.blogger.com/
5. http://wordpress.org

4. DICTATION

Online dictation exercises help students practice their listening skills with and give them a chance to interact, solicit feedback, and improve error correction.

A dictation exercise generally has a reader (either you or a recorded dictation) present a small text. Most teachers will read a dictation twice (first for students to write or type, and then again for students to confirm or make corrections). The text itself might be an already familiar text, in which case the dictation can serve as an assessment tool (students are looking for/writing down key words they should now know), or a dictation can serve as an introduction to new vocabulary (can students identify or guess at unknown words?).

A dictation exercise online can be done by instructing students to all write (or type) at the same time. In this case, students will write without sharing their answers. Then, as a second step, you may invite one of the learners to share his or her dictation on screen, and this can then prompt a discussion.

Alternatively, with a larger class, you may wish to have students type synchronously; for example, in a shared GoogleDoc. In this case, students will see, in real time, the different versions being created and can gain insights/make corrections based on shared student work.

Examples of Dictation Exercises on the Web:

1. https://www.englishclub.com/listening/dictation.htm
2. https://www.ixl.com/ela/

5. MODIFIED TPR

TPR, or Total Physical Response, was a method of instruction created by James Asher that allowed students to learn language through a chronological event filled with gesture and movement, and gave learners a chance to be silent while observing language.

While some teachers might think that online teaching prevents this sort of face-to-face delivery, most veteran online teachers recognize that lessons require a teacher to be seen, at least during key moments of conversation. Thus, in these face-to-face moments, an online teacher must practice being overtly expressive with his or her hands and face. TPR is particularly useful when learners need visual cues to reinforce new words and expressions.

Method #1: Use movements to represent common words or expressions. For example, you could use a thumbs up to represent *Good* job, and a finger scratching the head to suggest *I don't know*.

Method #2: Use movements to represent abstract words. Consider how you might visually represent (with your body, hands, and face) the words *freedom*, *friendship*, *love*, or *happiness*.

Method #3: Use movements to express a time sequence. When you tell a story or relate a sequence, pay attention to the beginning, middle, and end, and change locations or movements accordingly. For example, can you think of movements for a story about someone writing a book, then going to a door, and then driving a car?

Method #4: After any of these examples of modified TPR, you can ask students to perform an action by stating the vocabulary word. Conversely, you can perform an action and have students say the word out loud. ("What am I doing? That's right; I'm driving.")

Pictures are often used to help facilitate TPR activities.

6. RANDOMIZE PARTICIPATION

Many teachers struggle to have students participate in class. There are many reasons for this in a language classroom. One way to encourage speaking is to randomize participation.

This can be done by assigning a number to each student, or by using a physical or digital spinner. Multiple online spinners or apps are available to randomize student participation. While digital spinners are good for spontaneous question and answer periods, one problem in the language classroom is that students often feel like they do not have enough time to answer a question. Thus, you may wish to have all the questions made available, and have students go through and answer the questions to themselves privately. Then students can be randomly assigned to answer the question out loud or by typing. Alternatively, you can have students assigned to specific questions, and give each student time to reason through an answer. Students can then be called on according to number (ascending or descending) or can even volunteer to speak when they feel they have prepared an adequate answer. Above all, you must recognize that in an online language classroom, getting students to participate evenly is a major challenge that you must think through. Please note that discussion blogs, writing prompts, and wikis allow for asynchronous participation.

7. READ-ALOUD

While this activity has been called by many different names, the basic concept behind a **read-aloud** is to give learners the chance to comprehend a reading by having it spoken out loud, by you. Read-aloud activities give opportunities for you to teach different learners a variety of strategies for reading, listening, and speaking.

Before a read-aloud, learners may be given a sheet of questions to answer, a list of vocabulary words to look for, or another language task. Here are some tips for a successful teacher-directed read-aloud:

- Choose a story that students love or relate to.
- Be sure that every student has the story sent to them digitally ahead of time.
- Read in a dynamic voice.
- Pause often and stimulate interest by asking students to predict.
- Have students read along to various parts, especially exciting or interesting parts.
- If possible, watch a movie clip version after you have read a particular chapter.

8. READING CIRCLES

In a read-aloud (see activity #7), you are the voice reading to students. In a reading circle, students have a chance to be voices themselves. There are many techniques to encourage student participation. Consider the following:

- **Choral Reading** – All participants read out loud and all together.
- **One by One and Sentence by Sentence** – Each student reads a sentence in turn.
- **Dramatic Reading** – Ask students to focus on an emotion or feeling (either as a group or individually).
- **Physical Response Reading** – Have students describe and act out physical actions and movements.
- **The Leader and The Choral Response** – Have the leader read one sentence; then the group echoes back that sentence (or the group might read the next sentence).

Alternate back and forth between the leader and the group reading a sentence out loud.

- **Male and Female Roles or Turns** – All the women read one sentence and then the men read the next, or take turns reading the dialog for women and for men.
- **Fill in the Missing/Silent Words** – The leader reads out loud and pauses in the sentence for the group to fill in the words that are the focus of vocabulary or pronunciation practice.
- **Silent Reading** – Everyone reads a paragraph or page silently and then questions are asked about the reading or vocabulary, etc.
- **Listen and Read** – Participants watch part of the movie and then read the same portion of the story in the book (this is a good review and a way to cover more difficult passages twice for better comprehension).
- **Read and Listen** – Participants read a passage in the book and then review the same part in the movie (this is a good way to focus on listening to dialog, vocabulary, grammar, and comprehension).
- **Read and Discuss** – The leader can ask questions about the reading or how the participants feel about a topic or idea presented in the book or movie.
- **Read and Write** – Participants can write book reports or short essays in a class environment.
- **Share Your Favorite Part** – After students listen to (or read) the book, have them share their favorite part and explain why they like it. This will be good speaking practice, and can even spark discussion if other students are allowed to ask clarifying questions.

9. EVEN AN APPLE ACTIVITY

Veteran language teachers are able to take an object, a group of images, an article, or a video and turn it into an opportunity for students to use a language. The idea is that any item—even a picture of an apple—naturally invites students to produce language. When shown objects or videos, basic students generally describe what they see, while at more advanced levels, students might make inferences or share opinions about the item.

In general, when you find an interesting item for students to look at or think about, you can use reading, writing, listening, or speaking activities to support it.

Writing: You can have students write down as many words as possible based on the item, create a story based on the item, or craft questions for other students to answer about the item.

Reading: Have students do a web search about the item, or prepare a reading that explains information about it. A jigsaw or information gap activity can often be created based on any reading the you prepare.

Listening: Ask students to listen to a short passage based on a picture, video, or reading; or, if using a video, perform a cloze passage exercise. Alternatively, students can listen to other learners in the classroom discuss the object.

Speaking: Have students make predictions from a video, or make inferences about an object. You can create a series of questions that students can respond to individually, in pairs, or in groups.

You might be surprised at how much students want to describe something as simple as an apple when given the chance and given supporting activities. Anything can be an opportunity to teach a language.

10. ONLINE LIBRARY OR LINKED WEBPAGE

Over time, you will start collecting a number of websites and resources that are useful for students. Consider placing these valuable resources (and perhaps instructions on how to use them) on a linked webpage to serve as a sort of online or digital library. Your online library might include your favorite student links for reading, listening, writing, speaking, grammar, and pronunciation. You can find short stories that students find compelling, video clips that explain how to pronounce difficult sounds, and so forth.

You might also want the page to include language apps, language websites, dictionaries, translation tools, and language games. These resources can help motivate students to practice outside of their assigned work, and can make them more and more connected to the online language learning communities. You might invite students to share "treasures" that they find on their own, encouraging them to tell you their favorite websites, games, and activities for learning a language. You might be surprised at just how much your students can teach YOU.

Part II: Warm Up Activities

"What seems hard now will one day be your warm up."

A proper warm-up activity can accomplish several purposes. First of all, warm-up activities can bridge old to new information, thus leading students to make a connection between previous lessons and a new theme or concept. In its most basic form, a warm-up activity helps students remember what they know (by stimulating the recall of prior knowledge) and then build upon it.

A warm-up activity can also introduce new information in a way that serves as an attention-getting device, which is why warm-ups are sometimes called attention getters.

That stated, a warm up should not just gain students' attention but direct that attention to an appropriate target; thus it can and should also serve to bring students a broad view of the topic that will be introduced later in the lesson plan. Good warm ups are ideally intriguing to learners, at least in the sense that they can give information in a way that invites curiosity and elicits prediction. Because of this, the use of visuals, question prompts on the board, or small videos are common.

Another way to think about warm ups is through the use of the idiomatic expression to prime the pump. This old time expression means to stimulate growth by providing a small catalyst. In the past, water would easily not come out of old, dry well pumps, so a common technique was to place a small amount of water down the mouth of a dry pump to activate it. In a similar way, a warm up is a small activity that "primes the pump." In other words, a little activity, just like a little water, activates background knowledge, intrigues students, and gives them access to what they already know (the 'well' of their knowledge).

Warm ups often naturally lead into objective discussions, which can further inspire students to consider what skills they will gain through the completion of the lesson.

11. CURIOSITY WARM UP

Just as speakers often begin their speeches with jokes, stories, or questions to get their audience interested in their topic, teachers need to find ways to begin their lessons that grab students' attention. What better way to do this than by invoking their curiosity?

Use activities such as riddles, guess who's, or jeopardy-type games to get students curious about the topic and excited to learn more.

For example, if you have been learning about different occupations, you can begin with a series of riddles about occupations.

> *I work in an office.*
> *I answer the phone and take messages.*
> *I type fast.*
> *Who am I?*
> (A secretary)

Similarly, you might create a Jeopardy game that has questions ranked in order from easiest to hardest with different categories related to your theme, and then you could play the game throughout the lesson.

Students can practice their listening and speaking skills by playing a "Guess who?" game in which they have to figure out the person by only asking "yes/no" questions.

Each of these activities can be a great warm up to invoke curiosity and get your students ready for the lesson.

12. GOAL/PRIZE WARM UP

Who doesn't enjoy winning a prize? Games can get the competitive juices flowing and excite students for the lesson ahead. Prizes could be points awarded to be "redeemed" at the end of the class or the unit, or they could even be digital rewards such as online Amazon gift cards. However, the prize could just be the satisfaction of being the winner of the game. This will depend on your students and your teaching style.

Games can be as simple as giving students a topic and a time limit to write as much as they can. As a variation, you might give students a topic and have them speak for one minute on that topic, or you can have students look at a picture and write a story in 5 minutes.

Here are some ideas:

- Write as many colors as you can. You have one minute. Go.
- Write everything you remember about Mrs. Smith in the story we just read. Go.
- Write down the names of the seven people in the story. Go.
- Write down the definitions of the words I say aloud. Ready? Let's begin.

Students can then share whatever they produce (a list, a paragraph, a story). In some cases, it might be appropriate for them to vote on a winner.

13. REVIEW TO CONNECT WARM UP

Good teaching is about helping students to make connections. Reviewing vocabulary from the last class that connects to a story or assignment in this class is a great way to conduct a warm up. For instance, if you taught nouns the day before and are teaching verbs today, you might review the nouns by having students identify them in sentences, and then ask them to show the action (verb) that the nouns perform.

Teacher (*shows picture of a dog*): The dog.
Student: The dog.
Teacher: Good. Now remember today's vocabulary. (*shows picture of a dog walking*): The dog...?
Student: The dog is walking.

In this last example, acting out the actions (the verbs) reinforces the meaning and puts them in a context that is more memorable for students. This model of instruction is sometimes referred to as **interleaving**, which means that you connect two concepts. Similarly, if you teach nouns today and adjectives tomorrow, you can continue to interleave your lesson. If you think of each topic as a letter, you could state that you connect a to b, b to c, c to d, and so on.

14. STORY WARM UP

A good story is an excellent way to get students interested and excited about their learning. Using a story in your warm up, and then breaking it down throughout the lesson, brings continuity to the lesson.

For example, begin by reading the story of "The Three Little Pigs."

Besides the obvious use of testing comprehension, you can also break it down to teach different concepts like past tense verbs (*huffed*, *puffed*, *blew*, *knocked*, *ran*, *danced*, etc.), story sequencing, question words (who, what, when, where, why), and even classic retell, where students retell the story in their own words.

There are many different story formats as well. You could use picture books, graphic novels, or shortened versions of classic stories. Keep them short, so they are accessible and not too overwhelming. These are used to pique students' interest, and can also be used to teach story elements, text features, and context clues. The possibilities are endless!

15. WHY BEFORE WHAT WARM UP

This activity invites you to consider sharing with students the WHY of instruction before you begin with the WHAT. Let us explain the theory behind this and then get into how you might accomplish this as an online teacher. First, consider the famous quote by Lewis Carroll in the story *Alice in Wonderland*, where the Cheshire cat asks Alice where she is going:

Cat: Where are you going?
Alice: Which way should I go?
Cat: That depends on where you are going.
Alice: I don't know.
Cat: Then it doesn't matter which way you go.

In the education world, this is often referred to as your teaching objective. You need to know WHERE you are going (WHAT you are teaching), and WHY you are teaching it. It's important for you to have a clear objective in mind for what you want the student to be able to do by the end of the lesson—but letting your student in on the WHY they are learning this objective is even more important.

In order to teach why before what, consider giving your students what we call **future authenticity** by telling them *how they will be able to use this information in the future.* Have them imagine where and when they might use specific language forms.

For example: *Imagine you are at the airport in a foreign country, and you need to get a taxi and give the driver directions to your hotel. Would you know what to say? Today you will learn how to do this.* Or give your students the objective: *We are going to learn how to talk about our families* and ask them to tell you when and where this might be useful.

Help them to understand WHY they are learning something before they actually learn it.

16. FOUR PICTURES, ONE WORD WARM UP

For this warm up activity, find four pictures that relate to one vocabulary word, especially a vocabulary word that is essential for a future reading or theme. (For example: a basketball, a soccer net, a referee, and a swimmer. The vocabulary word is *sports*.)

You can find pictures that align with the vocabulary words you will be using in your lesson or that students will be reading in a story that day. This is a fun way to introduce vocabulary and get students prepared for the lesson at the same time. Later, when they are reading the story or you come across the vocabulary word, you can show them the four pictures again to remind them of the word's meaning.

As a variation, you might find four pictures that allow you to share a story, or find four pictures that allow students to compose their own. Basically, the four pictures activity should invite students to connect the visuals, which stimulates critical and creative thinking.

In this example, students are learning about animal homes. You show one picture at a time, and the answer would be *cave.*

17. WRITTEN PROMPT: QUESTION OR STATEMENT

The use of a question or statement can be a powerful way to introduce a theme online. While the concept is simple, finding the right question or statement to evoke participation is not so simple. When you use this technique, make sure that you are inviting students to respond to something that directly targets the information you will be trying to teach later on.

Often, a quote that invites a difference of opinion or multiple angles can stimulate conversation. For example, using a quote from a famous individual can invite a discussion about what people know about that individual:

Q: What do you know about Martin Luther King, Jr.?

Or you might ask how learners feel about a particular quote from that individual:

Q: Do you agree or disagree with Dr. King's statement?

Sharing a quote can also lead into a prediction exercise about future content:

Q: What do you think this quote has to do with what we will talk about today?

It can also be tied to past content:

Q: What does this have to do with what we discussed yesterday?

In other words, when you display a quotation or a question, what often follows are a series of follow-up questions to help students start talking and thinking about the theme. Invite students to respond using a discussion board, live chat box, or in person during a face-to-face session. In a live session, give positive feedback for those who are willing to speak. While this warm up may only be a few minutes long, it can serve to engage students into thinking about the theme and give you information about what students already know.

Consider the following example themes and sample prompts that might accompany them:

Level	Theme	Prompt (Question or Statement)
Basic	Family	What makes a family?
Intermediate	Family	What do you love (and hate) about your family?
Advanced	Family	A family isn't always about blood. Agree or disagree.
Basic	Food	What are your favorite foods?
Intermediate	Food	"All you need is love. But a little chocolate now and then doesn't hurt." Charles M. Schulz
Advanced	Food	"There are people in the world so hungry that God cannot appear to them except in the form of bread." Mahatma Gandhi

18. PICTORIAL PROMPT

While it is commonly stated that "a picture is worth a thousand words," in the online language world, pictures elicit a thousand words. A good picture can help to begin a class conversation and have students immediately engage in thoughtful discussion. Just as with a written prompt, a pictorial prompt involves you asking a lot of questions about the picture to lead students into a discussion about the current lesson.

A good pictorial prompt can be displayed online or printed out and shown next to you as you instruct online. In either case, it should be large enough for all students to see, and often has something unusual or interesting to talk about.

You may begin by asking, "What do you see?" or ask a more specific question, such as "What problems do you see in this picture?" or "Why do you think this boy is sad?" A good picture often has multiple answers, and you can ask for a wide variety of opinions.

When students are answering, you may have to provide key vocabulary to explain certain visual items ("Does anyone know what this is? It's called a rainbow. Let me write that on the board."). Remember that you may wish to let students write down their answers, or discuss in pairs or in groups, before they speak to the entire class or to you.

In this picture, some basic questions might be:

- Describe the people in the picture.
- What else do you see in the picture?
- Where are they? What is the girl doing?
- What is the woman doing?

Intermediate questions might be:

- Tell me what they will do next. What could the woman be teaching the girl?
- When you go grocery shopping, which fruits and vegetables do you buy the most?
- Do you eat enough fruits and vegetables?
- How often do you eat them?

Advanced questions might be:

- Compare this kind of shopping with online shopping. How are they similar? How are they different?
- Parents often take their children shopping. What benefits does a children gain by going shopping with an adult?

19. SCRAMBLED SENTENCES

For this activity, you must have a reading in your future instruction. Choose a paragraph of any length (smaller for beginning students and larger for advanced). Scramble the sentences using sentence-scrambling software:

http://www.altastic.com/scramblinator/
https://www.edu-games.org/sentence-games/sentence-scrambler.php

Unscrambled:
I love dogs.
Dogs catch frisbees.
I love dogs that catch frisbees.

Scrambled:
dogs. / I / love
Dogs / frisbees. / catch
catch / dogs / that / frisbees. / I / love

Have students individually, in pairs, or in groups, put sentences in the correct order. For convenience you may wish to number each sentence (in a random order), so you can discuss the correct order after students are done.

After students assemble the scrambled sentences and there is a class consensus on the correct order, ask students what they think the reading will be about. Pre-teach vocabulary by using the words present in the sentences, or get students to share their thoughts about what they have read so far. If possible, you may wish to put a full version on display to show the correct order.

20. DRESS UP

The online world is a visual one, so while this activity can feel a bit risky, it has the added benefit of being one of the most visually arresting.

The activity itself is simple. If you are talking about a cowboy and reading about a cowboy, why not dress up like a cowboy? When performing this activity, you can do several linguistic activities at once. You can ask students about vocabulary and invite them to guess at some of the features of the costume (*These are **spurs**; this is my **ten-gallon hat***). You can also invite students to guess what the theme might be.

You might also want to act out a small skit to help the students understand some of the upcoming content.

21. BOX PROPS

For teachers who might not feel comfortable putting on a costume, nor have the time and resources to find one, a more feasible alternative is the use of box props.
For this activity, bring in a box of items that relate to the theme, pull out each item, and have students discuss each item and then the items as a whole.

For example, imagine you are teaching about food or cooking. You might gather simple items from the kitchen, or perhaps a number of simple food items like fruit. You can pull out items and ask students to guess the theme, or conversely, ask them to identify as many items as they can. They could also describe the items that you pull out of the box, or write down as many words as each object conjures up in their imagination.
Sometimes a single prop is all that is necessary to intrigue students and to introduce a theme.

22. WARM-UP WITH DIALOGUE

Invite students to listen to a dialogue. The dialogue can be read by you, pre-recorded by you and another person, or can be a random clip from a movie or TV show. Tell students to listen carefully for key vocabulary and ideas. Have students summarize the dialogue in writing via upload or discussion board.

As with all warm ups, the dialogue should include key vocabulary and themes for the lesson, and should invite students to think, talk, and predict.

A: How may I help you?
B: I can't find a book I need.
A: Did you check the online catalog?
B: Yes, I did, and it was listed.
A: Was it on the shelves?
B: Well, I didn't see it.

A: Maybe it's checked out. But let me help you look.
B: Thank you very much.

23. RANKING ACTIVITIES

pg. 76

In a ranking activity, you ask students a series of questions that they either disagree or agree with, or anything else that can be ranked (height, number of brothers and sisters, number of countries you have visited, number of shoes you own).

For the classic agree/disagree ranking activity, there are several ways to have students respond. In the flipped classroom, have students hold up a thumbs up or for agree, a thumbs down for disagree, or invite students to write a number from one to ten. You might also consider using www.plickers.com or clickers in order to poll a group. Sometimes teachers will literally ask students to line up and discuss.

In online environments you might be able to use polling software (some learning management systems or video conferencing systems feature polling). Questions should naturally invite students to differentiate themselves from each other by physical characteristics, personality, hobbies, beliefs, and preference.

- Who has a birthday closest to today? Farthest from today?
- Who has the most pets?
- Who can ride a bicycle?
- Who is the tallest?

24. VALUE LINES

pg. 76

Value Lines is a ranking activity for which you show a graphic and asks students to respond to the graphic. It is most commonly used when discussing preferences, and is used for flipped classroom and synchronous face-to-face classes. A value lines activity provides a way for students to respond quickly. Hold up the graphic, ask a question, and then wait for students to respond (in online environments, you will likely have polling software to help you collect the data).

For example, for a theme on food, you could have students respond to the following by selecting a number from one to ten (1 means you agree a lot, 2 agree a little, 3 neither agree nor disagree 4 disagree a little, and 5 disagree a lot). If you do not have polling software on your learning management system, you might look into online polling such as www.plickers.com.

- I love broccoli.
- I love ice cream.
- I eat a lot in the morning.
- I want to eat better.
- I eat when I'm happy.
- I eat when I'm sad.

25. OFF TOPIC-ON TOPIC WARM UP

This is an excellent activity to help students differentiate between on topic and off topic statements, to learn to generate on topic comments or questions, and to learn to ask partner-focused questions.

To illustrate, start with a simple theme, like *Going to the beach*. To perform this activity, show a picture of someone at the beach and then ask students to choose from four statements and the question "Which one is off topic?"

Which One is Off Topic?

- I love swimming in the summer.
- The beach is one of my favorite places to visit.
- Do you like to go to the shopping mall?
- My family loves to build sand castles at the beach.

After this, you might show a picture of someone at the grocery store or any other theme you wish. Ask students to come up with one statement that is on topic and one statement that is off topic, and then share the statements in a discussion board or chatroom.

This activity can be done with pictures or just written statements. The key is to see what students actually know about a topic, and to get them thinking about appropriate questions or comments they can make that pertain to the topic at hand.

26. TOILET PAPER CAPER

For the flipped classroom, the Toilet Paper Caper activity begins on a day students meet with you in person. In this case, stand at the door as students enter. As you stand at the door, when students enter, ask them the unusual question: "How many pieces of toilet paper do you need?" Do not tell students what the toilet paper will be used for. If a student asks, just tell them (cryptically), "Just take as many as you think you need." In an online classroom, you can do this the same way, except when you ask them the question, you tear off the number of squares they ask for and show it to them.

After everyone has entered (or "entered") the classroom, explain to students that the pieces of toilet paper indicate the amount of times a learner must participate in the classroom discussion (number of questions they must answer, number of comments they must make, etc.).

This game can be played many ways with different objects. For younger students, rather than using toilet paper, consider using small candies and ask, "How many do you need?" (You may need to put a limit on the number they can ask for).

In online environments, consider other kinds of motivational objects; some teachers use a physical jar for students, with a marble dropping into the jar every time they participate, so they can see their own efforts.

Part III: Guided Practice (Working with Students One on One)

"What a child can do today with assistance, she will be able to do by herself tomorrow."
– Lev Vygotsky

Guided practice comes from a theoretical principle which suggests that, generally, students can't simply do precisely what you say immediately after you say it. Students need time to consider, process, and practice the skills that you have invited them to master.

Guided practice often takes a portion of a complete, independent activity and has students work on a particular portion of that larger activity. For example, instead of working on an entire essay, students in a guided practice might work on paragraph writing. Similarly, students working on irregular verbs might focus their attention on only a few irregular verbs (all with a similar pattern), and then go on to another set of verbs (with another pattern).

Guided practice often takes shape as either teacher-led activities or group-directed activities, but in either case, the activities are structured to break down more difficult tasks. In teacher-led activities, it is wise to invite a variety of students to contribute. This can be done through question and answer, or even by beginning a sentence and inviting students to finish the sentence. Thus, in teacher-led events, you are often the language production "starter" and learners are the language production finishers. While trailing off may sound like a technique of an absent-minded professor, it is, in fact, a technique to engage students and allow them to both predict and create language.

In group-directed activities, select groups carefully by mixing high and low performers in each task. In this configuration, ensure that low performers are given the more difficult task. Studies have shown that when low performers are given the more difficult task, interactivity increases and allows for better overall performance within a group.

Guided activities should, ideally, invite students to think critically about the instruction and give them the requisite time to understand the instruction. A critical goal for guided practice is to get learners to a point where they can perform an independent task, or at the very least feel comfortable attempting one.

27. SINGLE SLOT SUBSTITUTION/DOUBLE SLOT SUBSTITUTION

While an overreliance on drills can lead to a lack of actual communicative competence, drills are often still used in synchronous online classroom settings. Substitution drills are some of the most common.

When you use a substitution drill, you read a sentence aloud. A single slot substitution means you invite a learner to exchange only one word for another per sentence. A double-slot substitution means that the student will substitute two words within a single sentence.

In online environments, students are often asked to repeat after you during live sessions, as you call on students one at a time. In flipped classroom environments, you can also choose students one at a time or have students repeat in choral fashion.

Single Slot

Teacher: The man is wearing a hat.
Student: The man is wearing a hat.
Teacher: a shirt
Student: The man is wearing a shirt.

Double Slot

Teacher: The dog is under the table.
Student: The dog is under the table.
Teacher: cat/chair
Student: The cat is under the chair.

Substitution drills are particularly effective with beginning learners who are handling new vocabulary.

28. BACKCHAIN DRILL

For longer sentences, or the sentences students struggle with, backchaining is an excellent drill. First, present the sentence to the learner. Then, in a backchain, you move from the end of the sentence, gradually increasing the number of words as you go along.

Sentence:
Yesterday, I went to the park and I saw dogs, cats, and some birds.

Backchain:
some birds.
and some birds.
cats and some birds.
dogs, cats, and some birds.
saw dogs, cats, and some birds.
I saw dogs, cats, and some birds.
and I saw dogs, cats, and some birds.
park and I saw dogs, cats, and some birds.
the park and I saw dogs, cats, and some birds.
to the park and I saw dogs, cats, and some birds.
went to the park and I saw dogs, cats, and some birds.
I went to the park and I saw dogs, cats, and some birds.
Yesterday, I went to the park and I saw dogs, cats, and some birds.

If you have a virtual whiteboard, you should continue to slowly add a word at a time, having students recite out loud each time a new word is added.

29. TRANSFORMATION DRILLS

Drilling is often considered a poor strategy to elicit advanced grammatical structures. However, transformation drills can help students to think beyond a single word. You can have students turn statements into questions, positive into negative answers, present into past sentences, and so forth.

Example 1
Teacher: The students love grammar.
Student: The students love grammar.
Teacher: The students love grammar. NOT
Student: The students do not love grammar.

Example 2
Teacher: The man is sad. (*show a picture*)
Student: The man is sad.
Teacher: The man is sad. QUESTION.
Student: Why is the man sad?
Teacher: The man is... (*show another picture*)

Student: The man is happy.
Teacher: The man is happy. QUESTION.
Student: Is the man happy?

Example 3
Teacher: The boy goes to school and sees his friends.
Student: The boy goes to school and sees his friends.
Teacher: The boy goes to school and sees his friends. PAST.
Student: The boy went to school and saw his friends.

30. COMPLETION DRILL

Another problem with drilling is that it can fail to produce authentic language. One type of drill, however, that allows for students to produce their own original work is the completion drill. In a completion drill, you read the beginning of a sentence, and the student finishes it.

Teacher: I love...
Student: I love apples.

You can complicate a completion drill by specifying a category.

Teacher: I love...
Student: I love apples.
Teacher I love...PERSON.
Student: I love...my mother.
Teacher: I love...HOBBY.
Student: I love basketball.

In an asynchronous classroom, you can create a series of sentence starters and invite learners to respond to a discussion board or a chatroom.

31. Q & A SESSION (THIS OR THAT/SINGLE ANSWER/OPEN ENDED)

After teaching a chunk of material, ask questions to understand what students have learned. One activity-based way to do this is to create a question and answer session. You can ask questions to discover if students understood the material or not. You generally should not ask the question, "Do you understand?" (since students will generally nod or say yes regardless of the level of their understanding). Rather, it is best to ask questions that require at the very least a response between two choices (this or that).

Teacher: Look at this sentence (*show slide*). Is it past or present?

Another way to conduct a question and answer session is to ask a question that requires a single response. In general, you should invite a single response that allows a variety of correct answers.

Teacher: What can you put on a table?

Finally, more advanced questioning involves open-ended questions. An open-ended question is a question that cannot be answered with a yes or no response. Open-ended questions are sometimes phrased as a statement.

Teacher: Tell me about the children in the photo.
Teacher: What is a perfect day?

Students would respond in a flipped classroom by raising their hands. In an online environment, learning management systems often allow students to virtually raise their hands. If this function is not available, call on students individually. Students could write or speak their answers.

Student 1: A perfect day is sunny.
Student 2: A perfect day is rainy with clouds.

32. DICTATION STATION

Dictation is done by reading to students, who then write or type what they believe they hear. In a synchronous online classroom, you could have one student show the other students what he/she wrote. After the student shares the response, the remaining students discuss if they have similar answers. In an asynchronous classroom, students can listen to a recorded text and submit their dictation exercises to you by uploading or via the discussion board. Answers can be provided afterward.

For dictation material, you can compose your own texts, or take a sample text from a book or online story. You might also choose small clips from movies, or even invite students themselves to dictate something.

Rather than having students write down what they hear, you could also invite them to listen and repeat, to see what details they can recall.

Another variation is to replace certain words with pictures or physical movements, so that students are required to guess the missing words.

33. FLASHCARD RECALL

Having students recall what they have learned is a key aspect of guided practice. Since guided practice involves helping students to gain mastery, it is practical to have students learn a certain amount of material through self-study. Using flashcards is a great way to have students remember individual words, but cards can be used in many other ways as well. Online teachers often use entire sentences as flashcards, with a missing word on the back of the flashcard.

Flashcards themselves can be created online or in-person. Online flashcards often show pictures or definitions. Online quizzing software such as Quizlet can be used to help learners practice material in a number of different ways.

Quizlet invites learners to memorize through various modes such as matching, spelling, and testing. In matching, students are asked to match words to definitions. In spelling, students are given a definition and then asked to write down what they hear. In testing mode, students are given a variety of question types to choose from such as multiple choice and true/false.

34. JEOPARDY

Jeopardy is a popular television game show whose format can be used to help students review key information. Jeopardy gives clues in the form of answers, meaning that the answers are given first, and contestants are asked to provide the questions.

When setting up a Jeopardy game, you'll want to create a number of "answers" that are ranked according to difficulty (100-dollar questions are easier, 1000-dollar questions are harder). There are also as many as six categories that you can set up when asking the questions, making this game a perfect tool to prepare students for an end-of-unit test.

For example, you might have categories such as *idioms*, *nouns*, *words that start with m*, or any other category that can help students demonstrate their knowledge of what has been covered in the class.

You may wish to split students into teams, or simply have students take turns answering questions. Jeopardy works best when you show and read out the question. If the team or individual answers correctly, then you can assign points to that team or student. The team or student with the most points wins!

You can create a Jeopardy game online using a number of different Jeopardy template creators. Here is one: https://jeopardylabs.com/

35. ALPHABET SOUP

Share the letters of the alphabet (A-Z) visually (either online or printed out). Ask your learners to write a word or sentence that begins with each letter. You may skip some letters, like X, if you choose. The words or sentences they choose should relate to the topic that they have just been studying.

For example, if students just finished watching a video about the Serengeti, they could complete sentences using the vocabulary and content of the video:

A: Antelopes run wild in the Serengeti.
B: Because they are killers, lions are called the kings of the jungle.
C: Cheetahs run faster than lions.
D: Danger is everywhere on the plains.

E: Elephants use their tusks to fight off predators.
F: Flies swarm the hippos.

You can alter the instructions to suit the level of the students. For example, you don't have to require a sentence to begin with the letter (for the letter E, "I love elephants" could be an acceptable sentence).

You can have all students complete each of the 26 letters, or assign a certain number of letters to each student.

This activity helps students to think about what they have recently learned or understood, gives them a chance to show their learning, and works especially well to prepare students for a quiz or test.

36. FILL-IN-THE-BLANK QUESTIONING

One excellent way to test student understanding is through fill-in-the-blank questioning. Begin sentences but then trail off and allow learners to complete them. This activity can be used to see if students have understood instructions such as a reading or dialogue.

Questions might be about:

Character: So the name of the lady was...
Place: And she lived in...
Detail: She didn't want to dance with Ivan because...
Inference: She probably thinks Ivan is...

When teaching activities such as vocabulary, you can begin sentences with:

Definitions: I love to climb trees and eat bananas. I am a...
The word: Monkeys are...
An antonym: The opposite of *day* is...

When teaching grammar, you can also use this technique:

Past tense: Give me an example in the past.
The girl...
The boy...
The elephant and the mouse...

Part III: Independent Practice (Getting Students to Go Solo)

"Practice makes the master."
– Patrick Rothfuss

Independent practices are simple in concept. The idea is that students have been given instruction, have gone through a number of activities, and are now ready to show their understanding. While independent practice is sometimes seen as an assessment activity, the two are not always one and the same. An independent practice may or may not be assessed by you for or to a test, final presentation, or project.

One of the difficulties for teachers in creating independent activities is that they often take a rather ordinary shape: essay, speech, or test. While each of these devices do allow students to practice their language production, independent activities can extend beyond these typical structures. In a project-based curriculum, researchers ask teachers to think outside the traditional box and think of unusual and fascinating ways to engage learners in language production.

The following activities attempt to introduce proper use of traditional independent practices, and then demonstrate activities that, with a little creativity from you, might provide engagement and authentic language production where there might otherwise have been a lack of interest from participants.

37. RIVER RUNS THROUGH IT

A scene in the iconic movie *A River Runs Through It* shows a disciplinarian father teaching his child the importance of precision in writing. He does this by asking his teenage son to write a full page on a subject, then a half page, and then half of that. Ultimately, his son learns how to carefully discard details and choose only the most essential parts of his essay.

As an online teacher, you can also give an assignment that invites a student to produce writing and then to summarize it once and again. Direct a student to respond to a prompt like this:

1. Describe the perfect day. Write for 5 minutes.
2. Describe that same perfect day. Write for 2 minutes. Keep all the essential details.
3. Describe the same perfect day. Write for 1 minute. Keep all the essential details.

This same activity can also be done in speaking.

Variation: Reverse River While some students have a difficult time summarizing, many have the reverse problem. They cannot write ENOUGH material. For these students, you may wish to do a "Reverse River." A reverse river means that you ask students to write a fourth of a page, then half page, and then a full page (or, write for 1 minute / then 2 minutes / then 5 minutes), having them add details and examples to their writing.

As you continue to stretch them to think of ways to expand their writing, students gain valuable insights on how to elaborate, to add evidence, or to simply keep going. Again, this can easily be converted to a speaking activity.

38. PREDICT/PRACTICE/PERFORM

The predict/practice/perform model invites students to create their own mini-lesson plans, which is useful in an online environment when you are teaching students to take responsibility for their own learning.

To begin, assign students a moderately difficult task, one that may take a few days but that is well within their current ability. A few examples of a task might be writing a birthday card, a recipe, a song, or a speech.

The students now divide the task into three corresponding parts. You may wish to have students upload something for each of the three parts:

Predict: At this stage, students consider what vocabulary, grammar, and information they need in order to complete the task.

Prepare: Students gather the necessary information, create drafts, and revise. This stage often involves collaboration with others.

Perform: Students complete and share the final task with you, classmates, or others.

Online teachers often find this is a useful pattern when preparing their instructions for any moderately difficult task or activity. Asking students to think through each of these three stages allows for more thorough work

39. ELEVATOR SPEECH (ONE MINUTE OF AMAZING)

An elevator speech is a prepared speaking activity that gives students the chance to speak about any topic for one minute. Students are given a prompt and then told to produce a small note card that will help them present a one-minute speech. To add in producing content freely, some online teachers have students write in the native language on one side and the target language in the back.

Students sometimes are asked to develop their own topics when doing elevator speeches. In this case, students imagine who they might meet in an elevator, and what they might want to say. They can imagine the most common conversations they might have so that they can practice small talk (family, friends, sports, education/vocation) to give them a comfort level with possible future events.

Elevator speeches serve to help students learn how to have impromptu conversations, but in a way that is structured and not nearly as scary. Students tend to feel proud of having spoken on a topic, and can also take pride in the fact that they have prepared extended conversation starters. You may have to help correct or revise elevator speeches, adding key vocabulary or grammatical help along the way.

40. RECOMBINATION STATION

Recombination refers to the ability to say a phrase or idea in different ways, and is an important skill in language learning.

One way to improve students' ability to recombine is to ask them to rewrite a story. After listening to or reading a story, students can share the story in their own words. In an asynchronous environment, have them upload a file or post to a discussion board.

Before they attempt to paraphrase, put up key vocabulary or pictures and invite students individually or collectively to think of different ways to say the same thing. However, remind students that it is often easier and more successful to restate an idea using different syntax instead of just trying to find synonyms for nouns and verbs. You might also (with students or beforehand) write down all of the key features of the story, and remind them to include all of them. Instruct students to use different vocabulary and grammar as they try to say things in their own words. Students will then produce a "recombined" version of the same story.

Afterward, you might ask students to check the original to see if they captured all of the main ideas or details of the story.

41. MR. BEAN

Mr. Bean is a show based on the British actor Rowan Atkinson's comical character of the same name. Mr. Bean is a beloved character who, although he is an adult, acts in childish (and humorous) ways. Because Mr. Bean uses very few words, it can be used to help students learn the valuable practice of narrating, describing, or listing. Students should first watch a series of short clips of Mr. Bean (perhaps 30 seconds each) and do the following possible activities:

> **Narrating**: Students take turns narrating the clip they just watched with a partner. Students can narrate in real time if they are advanced, or you might pause the clip and allow students time to narrate afterward.
>
> **Describing**: After each clip, students describe in writing what it was they saw. Then they can compare their writing to another student. Posting to a discussion board allows for easy side-by-side comparisons.
>
> **Listing**: Students are asked to write down as many of a particular category of words as possible. For example, students might be asked to write down all the verbs or nouns that they see.

This is a good recombination activity because students are forced to think of the vocabulary that they do know. In other words, if Mr. Bean is at a pool and goes down a slide, it is possible that while students do not know the word "slide" in the target language, they may be able to express the meaning in another way (*Mr. Bean goes down / Mr. Bean falls into the water*.) You might use this as an opportunity to teach new vocabulary, or let students explore the words that they do know collectively as a class.

42. TESTS

While a test or examination is something every teacher is familiar with, online tests are often tricky to create and administer. In some sense, bad tests are easy to give, but tests that actually measure knowledge are more complex. Here are a few things to keep in mind:

1. If you are an online teacher, you likely have access to a particular learning management system. If you do not, you might want to look into a free LMS (Moodle or Canvas, for example). These offer quiz and test options.

2. If you aren't given specific quiz and test makers by your school, you may need to look into online quiz and test makers. Many online tools allow for quizzes such as multiple choice, fill in the blank, drag and drop, and matching. Please consider both the strengths and disadvantages of each question type as it relates to the construct you are trying to measure.

3. Ensure that your tests measure the right construct. You must have in mind what a student should actually know and be able to perform. A proper test should measure the ability for that student to demonstrate knowledge of that construct. Thus, if the ability to use the passive voice is important for you, a test on simply *identifying* the passive voice is NOT enough. Asking students to produce the passive voice by completing sentences would be a better test of their ability to use and control the passive voice correctly.

4. Ensure that tests measure more than memory. You should keep in mind that a test, in particular a language test, should not just measure the memorization of facts but the student's ability to use language in real situations and in real time.

5. If you truly want to learn about testing, you should consider reading literature about how to best to construct a test. Make sure you pay attention to the terms *reliability* and *validity* and how they relate to test accuracy (*Teaching for Competence* by Sullivan & Higgins is an excellent resource).

43. COMPOSITIONS

Compositions, or written essays, are common devices that are easily given online to demonstrate learners' abilities. Generally speaking, modern writing theory suggests that essay writing is done over time, with multiple drafts, peer review, and conferencing for best results. This can also be done online, although it can be tricky if it involves having partners communicate with each other asynchronously. Students may need to become familiar with Skype, Facetime, Zoom, or other software that allows them to video conference with a fellow classmate.

Good writing assignments allow students time to engage in this kind of collaborative process, and thus, most writing theorists would suggest that you have a series of activities that lead up to the turning in of a final online paper. Here are a few ideas:

1. For writing essays, you generally give an assignment sheet that spells out due dates, different activities for pre-writing, writing, and revision. In the online world, this is done using learning management systems, wherein you can create announcements and pages that do much the same as an assignment sheet.

2. Model essays should certainly be presented at some point in the writing process, so students know what they are working towards, but you must consider when you want to show a model. It may be useful to show a model after the initial brainstorming and first rough draft.
3. When presenting a model, make sure that it demonstrates the types of language you want students to produce. Highlighting or underlining certain writing features in an essay can help students notice the language features you expect from them.

In addition to presenting a highlighted or annotated model, consider using a rubric that identifies key categories that you will use to evaluate the final product.

44. ONLINE PRESENTATIONS

An online presentation can be done both synchronously (live in front of you or group of students) or asynchronously (recorded and uploaded to you).

In general, it is an opportunity for students to demonstrate their ability to speak, present clear and organized ideas, and to show their persuasive or informative power to an audience. This mode also allows students to practice language strategies such as preparing notes and ideas, monitoring language output, organizing information, and controlling anxiety, all important skills for language production.

A presentation may be of varied lengths and complexities, but generally follow the same general principles.

As with a writing assignment, you should give students clear directions by creating an announcement or page within a learning management system.

One common online presentation format is the voiceover from PowerPoint or other presentation software. Another common way to do a presentation is for a student to record a video, with the PowerPoint in the background or other visuals as needed.

Use of a model and rubric is highly recommended. Rubric categories vary among language professionals, but may include such elements as:

- organization
- engaging content
- use of key vocabulary
- pronunciation
- body and voice
- persuasion
- ability to respond to an audience
- use of visual aids

If you can record past student presentations and demonstrate how they would score on a rubric, this can be an excellent way of demonstrating your expectations.

Part III: Listening Activities

"When you talk you are only repeating what you already know.
But if you listen, you may learn something new."
– Dalai Lama

The online teacher certainly considers well-planned listening activities and pays close attention to how they are structured and how they will be assessed.

The activities listed in this section will not generally show assessment or evaluative techniques, but rest assured that you should spend time thinking about how you would determine the success of each activity. Thinking with the end in mind will help to clarify your language objectives for each activity (in fact, some teachers only have very vague ideas about an objective at all).

Remember that a listening activity should not be a "break" in your instruction, but rather represents an opportunity for students to gain information, skills, and achieve goals. Since listening is generally given at the rate of speed of the speaker rather than the receiver, it can be more difficult than reading, which can be received at a learner's own pace. This difficulty can be overcome as you find techniques to help make listening activities more clearly understood.

You can break down listening activities and lighten the cognitive (learning) load of participants in several ways. For example, the simple technique of repetition cannot be overstated. If students are struggling with a listening activity, consider having them listen more than once and perhaps even discuss or write down what they heard. Another important way to break down listening activities is to pre-teach vocabulary, or to share key concepts ahead of time. Using prediction activities or follow-up questions also help to reinforce the information that students have received.

In some sense, a successful communicative teacher is not just one who is able to create strong language activities, but someone that creates a strong support system around each activity that is created.

45. THE MISSING HALF

Asking students to be accountable for information they have heard is a great way to improve their listening skills. For this activity, divide an article in two, and assign the first half of the students, the Student A group, to read the first half of the article, while the second half of the students, the Student B group, reads the second half of the article. Since you may not be in front of the students to monitor them during this activity, it might be a good idea to create two separate documents, each with one half of the article, to keep students from reading the half they were not assigned. You can provide separate links on your course platform, or email the Student A group a link to download their half of the article, and email the Student B group a different link.

After students have read the article, invite the Student A partners to look for Student B partners (and vice versa). Have students read aloud the paragraph to their partner, or record themselves reading their half of the article aloud and share the recording with their partner.

Give each student comprehension questions that relate to the half of the article they heard their partner read aloud, and ask them to share their answers with their partner for feedback.

46. HEADBANDS (A MODIFIED VERSION)

In a face-to-face classroom, to carry out this activity you would place the name of a famous celebrity on a headband, making sure that the person does NOT know what name appears on his or her own headband. For example, if studying a unit on sports, you might write a number of famous sports celebrities on the headbands like Maria Sharapova, Mohammed Ali, or Lionel Messi. Students then walk around the room and look at each headband, with clear instructions not to say the name of the celebrity. Students take turns asking one another questions in order to figure out their identity, while other students give helpful clues. This activity can introduce a theme, help students to work on question formation, and give opportunities for students to respond to questions.

In an online classroom you can do this in a modified way. You don't have a "headband" on, but instead you have the name of a famous celebrity or person in mind, and the student has to guess who it is by asking you questions (in the exact same manner as if they were wearing the headband).

In this way, they are still working on question formation, you are still giving helpful clues without disclosing the person's identity, and they are still thinking critically to come up with the answer. Teacher and student can take turns asking questions and being the one who answers questions

47. TRUTH OR FICTION

Instruct students to write something true but surprising about themselves. (Example: *I once ate an entire cake by myself* OR *I have visited twelve different countries*). Tell students that the more unusual it is, the better. Then, students should write two untrue statements—they can also be unusual, but should at least be plausible so as to trick other students.

Next, have students record themselves sharing each statement, or have them share the statements in a live videoconference. The other students listen and have to guess which of the three statements are true (truth) and which are false (fiction). Students can post their guesses, or they could submit them via an online poll and the results shared with everyone. After students have had a chance to vote, the speaker can reveal the truth.

This activity can help learners pay attention to not only the words of a speaker, but to tone and body language.

48. CLOZE PASSAGE

To understand the basics of using a "cloze" passage, see Top Ten Activities.

To practice listening with a cloze passage, you can prepare a cloze passage using the lyrics of a popular song, a movie clip, or even an article or a poem that you read aloud to the students during a live session or in a recorded video. Conversely, you can have students listen to a recording of the same passage.

Students will listen and complete the cloze passage as they listen. If you are reading aloud, you might stop or slow down when a word must be produced in the passage. Sometimes you will provide the word more than once, or read each sentence twice before moving on.

If using a recording, such as a video or a song, you may want to make the task easier by presenting it multiple times (or pausing at the right time). Also consider playing the entire song or passage through once before repeating it and having students complete the cloze.

If given in an asynchronous format, students will likely be able to have control of the recording. You might want to tell them how to pause a recording, or to go back and listen again when they are not sure what was said.

49. DRAW A PICTURE

Instruct students to draw a picture, according to your specific directions. You could record a video of the directions or provide them during a live session.

During a live session, be sure to have the directions written out in advance so you can give the directions the same way each time. You should also have a picture to show students after their attempts at drawing according to your instructions.

When using a recorded video, you may want to provide the picture as a separate video or as a post which students can see only after they have completed their own drawings. See the template for an example of a picture with directions.

As a variation, several similar pictures can be shown on the screen or posted in a discussion forum. Then students hear you describe one of the pictures and are asked to identify the correct picture. They can do so by raising their hand in a live session, or posting their choice in the discussion forum. You might then invite them to describe any of the other pictures that were not described.

50. PERFORM THE INSTRUCTION (FETCH IT!)

Ask students to perform a task such as making a paper airplane, following your specific instructions. Record the instructions in advance or give the instructions on camera during a live session. When giving the instructions, make sure to not use any gestures or other visual cues that would help students understand what to do without listening. Students who are able to perform the task correctly following the instructions are rewarded for good listening.

One way to make this activity more fun is to use incorrect visual cues while giving the instructions. For example, you might tell students to place the paper for their airplane on their chairs, while you place it on your head, or on the floor. If you want to know how well students followed your spoken instructions instead of following what they saw, you could have students record themselves while they complete the task. Students who followed the words instead of the actions are rewarded for good listening.

51. GUEST SPEAKER

Invite a guest speaker who might be of some interest to the students. Before the speaker comes, invite students to write down questions ahead of time that they want to ask the guest speaker, and then have students ask those questions during or after the guest speaker's presentation. You may wish to tell the guest speaker ahead of time what questions the students have.

If possible, have students join a live session with the guest speaker, where they can ask their questions either by speaking or by typing in a chat box. If students cannot join a live session, have them watch a recording of the guest speaker and then submit their questions on social media or via email. Your guest speaker may be able to provide the answers by replying directly to students, or you may want to compile a list of questions and have the guest speaker provide the answers to you, which you then share with the students.

52. POST A VIDEO ON SOCIAL MEDIA

With the advent of the internet, language learning has never been easier. Connecting to others by posting a video can be a great way to accomplish two goals: First, it will force your students to prepare and perfect a certain amount of language, which is definitely an important skill to acquire. Second, it will allow others who speak the language (or who are learning it just like your students) to find each other. Think of it as a homing beacon to like-minded adventurers.

You might ask students to post a video about a certain topic, or let them choose what they want to talk about. The important thing is that they are preparing and producing language. For more advanced students, you could have them post a video of them interviewing someone else in the target language. Make sure to have them give you the link to the video if you are not following them on social media. If your students are wary about posting videos on their own social media, you can have them post the videos in a discussion forum or in a closed Facebook group that is just for your class.

Part V: Reading Acticities

"Reading brings us unknown friends"
– Honoré de Balzac

Reading activities teach not only online teachers how to read to students in a variety of ways, but also how to get students themselves to use a variety of techniques.

While many of your learners may think that reading simply involves going word by word and sentence by sentence, researchers now understand that reading is an involved process. Your job as a teacher is to read small stories, large stories, stories that learners see themselves in, and stories that stretch them to see things they have never considered. You will also help learners improve their reading skills by using techniques such as predicting, scanning, skimming, and asking questions.

In an online context, you must help learners understand texts that at first might seem impossibly difficult for them. Thus, your role in helping learners is to "unpack" written language by scaffolding. Scaffolding means helping break down otherwise difficult ideas by modeling, demonstrating key vocabulary and concepts, stepping back and asking questions, and then offering support as needed. Many online language teachers, in an attempt to scaffold, for example, pre-teach vocabulary, show pictures, stop reading entirely in order to explain a difficult passage in different words, and tell related stories to make more personalized or simpler connections.

Reading activities here in the next section vary between what you can do with your students during an online session and activities you can assign to students outside of that class time.

53. GUESS FROM A PICTURE OR TITLE/STORY GUESSWORK

Many students struggle to read difficult texts. This is especially true for those who read without using any pre-reading strategies. Teaching students to approach a reading by spending a few minutes "pre-reading" is an essential technique that online teachers can help students with when assigning a reading. Here are a few pre-reading strategies.

Guess from a Picture or Title

Choose an interesting picture (that relates to the story) and share the title. Ask students questions related to the picture and invite students to make predictions:

- What do you think the story is about?
- What do you know about X (*keyword in title/object in picture*)?
- Where/When do you think the story takes place?
- How do you feel about X (*keyword in title/object in picture*)?

Story Guesswork

This is similar to guessing from a picture or title, but requires a bit more work ahead of time. Rather than a single picture, you provide a series of pictures. To create interest, you might also read the first paragraph or section with students. This can be particularly successful if your intent is to make students interested in the article as a way of motivating them to read independently.

54. FIND A WORD, FIND A SENTENCE

In this reading exercise, you write a definition of a word (either on your screen or on a flashcard that you can hold up) without the word itself. Ask students to look for the word in the reading that has this particular meaning. This can be done as students are reading, thereby keeping them alert while reading.

Find the word: This word means "a shade of red."
Find the word: This word means "very happy."

For more advanced students, you can write questions or statements that challenge students to look for a specific sentence that answers the question.

Find the sentence: What is the man looking for?
Find the sentence: What are the two reasons that the woman is sad?

Displaying sentences in this fashion can help students increase their scanning skills, and can help students look for all kinds of important details. Using these techniques, you can also ask students to search for an interesting sentence, a main idea, a sentence that reminds them of another story, a sentence that the student disagrees with, and so forth.

Find the sentence that expresses the main idea of the story.
Find a sentence that reminds you of a personal story. Then share your story.
Find a sentence that makes you happy. Explain why it does.

55. READER'S OUTLINE Pg. 77

When assigning an online article, ask students to create an outline. An outline can be produced digitally and uploaded, or written down and then shared with you at the next online lesson.

An outline follows a typical format:

- main idea
    - subordinate idea
    - subordinate idea #2
- main idea #2
    - subordinate idea
    - subordinate idea #2
- main idea #3
    - subordinate idea
    - subordinate idea #2
    - subordinate idea #3

Preparing a template like the one above can help students know how many subordinate ideas you believe are in each paragraph or subsection. For further guidance, you might want to fill in some of the pieces of the outline for them.

1. main idea
    a. subordinate idea
    b. subordinate idea #2
2. Dogs are good hunters
    a. ears and nose are better than those of humans
    b. subordinate idea #2
3. Dogs are good pets
    a. subordinate idea

b. subordinate idea #2
c. subordinate idea #3

Outlines increase memory and give you a chance to assess a student's ability to identify supporting details.

56. CHARACTER MAP pg. 78

While outlines are good for informational articles, they don't work as well for a plot-driven story. One way to have your online learners write down details and share their knowledge of a story is by assigning them to complete a character map.

As always, choose a story that can be found online. Then, when you assign that story, tell students that they will have to choose a particular character in the story. You can create a list of characters they can choose from, or even assign characters to students to make sure they do not all choose the same one.

Then invite your learner to do the following:

1. Draw a picture of the character. If done online, you can have students upload the picture or choose a picture from an image search, looking for someone who might look similar to how they see the character.

2. Add information to describe the character's personality, struggles or problems, and physical characteristics. This can be a predictive activity as well, and you can ask students what you hope will happen to the character and/or what they think will happen to the character later on.

3. Students tend to do very well with this project when creating a character map using presentation software such as PowerPoint or Keynote. In this case, ask students to think of different topics for different pages, such as physical appearance, personality, main problem/conflict the character faces, favorite moment from the character's life.

57. PICTURE BOOK SUMMARY/SKITS

Creating a picture book online is a great way to have students relate stories to you or other members of your class. Since conversation can be difficult for learners, this gives each learner a chance to carefully prepare before they have to speak. Here are some basic rules:

1. Assign a book or short story for each student to read.

2. Ask students to create and upload a PowerPoint or Keynote presentation. The presentation will contain a series of pictures (no more than 10) about the story.

3. Tell students they will share something about each slide/picture. If you so choose, students might have a certain amount of text on each slide, or perhaps no text at all.

4. The students either record themselves or perform live during a classroom session. During the recording or performance, students will summarize the story to a partner or to you/the entire class.

If necessary, students may prepare small sentences on notecards. This allows students to first read and then present on what was read.

Skits

As an alternative to creating a picture book, article, or story, you could have students write a short skit based on the text. Students often love to act out the things they have read. They can record themselves performing the skit, and either upload it or perform it in the next class. You might ask them to post it on their social media!

Skits can come from a portion of the reading, the entire reading, or perhaps you can invite learners to write the "next chapter" of a particular story by asking them to consider what might happen next.

58. FOCUS ON A LITERARY TECHNIQUE

Online language teachers can learn a lot from literature teachers. Literature teachers often help teach students about metaphor, simile, symbols, rhymes, color imagery, description, setting, plot, allusion, or other literary devices.

As an online teacher, you might want to move away sometimes from just vocabulary and grammar and focus on a literary technique. When doing this, you may wish to consider a reading that highlights a unique/fun technique, one that elicits conversation. As you introduce a literary technique, you could do the following:

1. Explain the literary technique. Give some examples and define the term.

2. Ask learners to find the literary technique. You can highlight it within the story yourself, or have them look and highlight it themselves. If students are doing this asynchronously, one way to do this is by using a Google Doc or PDF (they can digitally mark these kinds of documents).

3. Discuss the way the author uses the technique within the context of the story.

4. Invite learners to use this technique themselves. For example, if you are learning about similes or metaphors, you could ask them to create their own.

In general, don't be afraid to teach good literary techniques as well as language. It may help students to learn to appreciate the beauty of another language, and will certainly help students to engage in reading.

59. MAPPING pg. 79

Doing a MAPP (with two p's) is especially useful when you are having students look at persuasive writing (such as advertisements).

To create a MAPP, here are a few tips:

1. Assign learners an online reading.
2. Ask learners to look at the reading in terms of four primary questions:

   M / Main Idea: What is the reading trying to teach?

   A / Audience: Who is this reading written for?

   P / Purpose: Why did the author write this?

   P / Personal Reaction: Why do you like or dislike this reading?

3. Invite learners to share their answers as a speaking activity (with a partner or with you), or as a written activity (upload/submit answers to you).

It is common for online teachers to assign more than one advertisement in order to have students see a contrast in audience or purpose. For example, one advertisement might be written for a young audience, while another advertisement might be written for a much older audience. After seeing such differences, learners can begin to identify key words or ideas that indicate a shift in audience or purpose.

60. SUMMARIZING/RANK ORDER EXERCISE pg. 80

A basic summary requires students to take an article or story and relate the main ideas in chronological order. While summarizing is a common activity in some countries, it is not a common practice in others. Thus, teaching learners to condense or summarize information can be an important educational activity. Asking students to find their own words to summarize can be equally challenging, but it will help students to learn how to simplify grammatical structures, create transitional words or phrases on their own, and use synonyms for key vocabulary.

<u>Rank Order Exercise</u>

Another way to have students recognize main ideas is to have them do a rank order exercise. In this activity, have learners read and take notes about ideas that seem important. Ask the following question to guide their note taking:

What are the most important ideas from this reading?

This could be, for example, the main themes of the reading, the morals of the reading, or just a list of the details themselves. It is best if a learner writes full sentences for each item he or she lists. Instead of saying child poverty for example, tell students to write, *Children often live in poverty in Brazilian favelas.* After learners have created a list of ideas, have them rank the ideas in order of importance. This might be done as a group or individually. Afterwards, you could invite a learner to share why the ideas were ranked in that order.

61. STOP AND PREDICT

This reading activity breaks up a text into different sections, and can be particularly useful when reading together with a student or class, when a text is long, or any other time when stopping might be considered necessary (like to introduce a cliffhanger). To use this technique, do the following:

1. Select a reading that is emotionally interesting or can be stopped at moments of high interest.

2. Stop students at a part of the reading that elicits a response to a question you ask, such as What do you think will happen next? or What do you want to happen next? Elicit one or more responses. If you have polling software, you can conduct a poll and share statistics. (It looks like almost all of you want John to ask Jessica for a date).

3. Continue reading the story and stop again at another moment. Repeat the questions.

This small technique allows you to keep the interest of the learners, and allows learners to feel that they are participating in the story.

62. ALPHABET READING AND QUESTIONS FROM A HAT

<u>Alphabet Reading</u>

This activity is an excellent one to help students review material; for example, when preparing for a quiz. While students are reading, invite them to verbally respond to each letter in the alphabet by sharing something vital about the reading. You might hold up a letter of the alphabet and have one or more learners respond. (For example, *Apricots were John's favorite fruit. Betty didn't like John.*)

<u>Questions from a Hat</u>

Another similar reading review activity is called questions from a hat. This activity, like alphabet reading, allows you to enlist the help of the students in coming up with ideas, and also challenges students to think critically about the reading.

Rather than writing all the test questions yourself, ask students to write or ask questions themselves. You could ask them, for example, to think of three questions each, and submit those questions to you. Then, on the day of the review, place the questions in a hat and draw them out in turn (or just share the questions online one by one).

This activity not only helps you to generate test question ideas, it will also allow students to think critically about the main ideas and important details of the content they are learning. In essence, you are getting your learners to think like a teacher!

63. WORD SEARCH

Create a word search or crossword puzzle based on the vocabulary words of the reading. A word search has rows and columns of letters. Words may appear horizontally, vertically, diagonally, and go both forwards and backwards. For a free word search generator, try http://www.puzzle-maker.com/WS/

Word searches are especially useful in two particular contexts. First, as a review tool—when students need to review the reading vocabulary (for a quiz or as part of a larger assignment), a word search can help students to recognize the words necessary to be successful on the quiz or assignment. Additionally, word searches reinforce correct spelling.

Another context, however, is a sponge activity. Since some students are faster than others at completing a task, a word search can often help reinforce the ideas of the lesson and allow faster students some opportunity for additional practice. If you have a particularly quick student, it can be nice to have an online assignment that includes a word search for when there is extra time.

Part VI: Writing Activities

"Writing is thinking on paper."
– William Zinsser

Writing activities can come in many different forms. For the online language teacher, writing activities often represent a chance for students to finally show off their learning and respond to the material you have presented. Thus, writing activities are windows into your learners' mind, giving you a chance to assess what students know and think (focus on meaning), as well as how well they are performing (focus on form). These two paradigms, focusing on meaning and form, fundamentally change the kinds of activities you create when assigning writing activities.

Those who focus on meaning are generally interested in how well their learners communicate their own ideas, and they often spend time creating activities that give learners time to generate, germinate, and expand ideas. On the other hand, for the "focus on form" teacher, writing activities can represent opportunities for learners to follow particular linguistic principles. These teachers can create activities that elicit the proper use of writing conventions or grammatical rules.

The activities presented in this section can be used for both paradigms, and often, with just a little imagination, can be used and modified in ways that can simultaneously accomplish a teacher's requirements to pay attention to both meaning and form.

Notice that many of these activities require you to think of a prompt in order to be successful. A prompt can be a question, a statement, or even a picture or object that students must respond to. Writing is often enhanced by your ability to inspire students to WANT to write, which can be achieved with the quality and interest level of the prompts you create.

When focusing on meaning, try to ask questions that are all based on a similar theme. This will activate background information. For example, if the class will be talking about the beaches of Hawaii for their next lesson, try to ask 4-8 questions that will encourage students to think about Hawaii (animals, people, food, places). When focusing on form, ask questions that will allow learners to respond to that form. For example, when teaching the past tense, ask learners to describe what they did last week, last year, over the summer, and so forth.

64. DOUBLE IT: I LIKE X, BUT I HATE Y

It's easiest to get students writing (or speaking) when you find things they are passionate or excited about. Generally when you discuss things they like or hate, you are on the right track.

This can be done by saying:

> I like ______, but I hate ______.

After producing a number of these pairs, follow up with this question:

> Why do you like _____?

After an initial discussion, have students choose one of the statements to write about. Remind them to expand their writing by explaining WHY they like or hate something, and possibly telling the story behind it.

> *I like pizza, but I hate fish.*
>
> *I like pizza because it was a rare treat for us to have pizza. I have fond memories of eating pizza and drinking soda with my family while playing games. I hate fish because when I was young, we ate fish every night, and one night I became violently ill. Ever since then I have not been able to eat fish.*

I like reading, but I hate writing.

My mom used to read to me every night. During the summer months we had special library trips each week, and the smell of the library always brings me back to my childhood. I loved listening to my mom read with different voices, and I couldn't wait to read out loud just like her. I hate writing because I want the stories to be already written. I can't think of interesting ideas like the stories I read, and it frustrates me.

(This can also be a speaking activity)

65. SENTENCE STARTERS

Sometimes all students needs to get their writing going is a simple sentence starter. Sentence starters will be different depending on what type of writing you are encouraging learners to do.

For analyzing writing:

- I like how the author...
- A golden line for me is...

For predicting:

- I think...
- If____ , then____...

For evaluating:

- I like/I don't like _____ because...

For discussion or conversation starters:

- I need help with...
- I'm curious about...
- What do you think would happen if...

66. SWITCH

This activity is aptly named because students will need to switch topics often. To perform this activity, you will need a number of different prompts or questions. Tell students a specific time limit they will be given to answer each prompt and that when they hear you call out "Switch!", they will move to the next question or prompt.

Questions might be personal or impersonal, based on a reading or lecture, or even based on a grammatical principle you want learners to demonstrate.

Questions and prompts can be read aloud to students, written on the screen, or held up for them to read. Once you say go, give students the allotted time to give an answer, perhaps reminding them when time is almost up (or using an online stopwatch to help them keep time themselves).

When you say "switch," students stop writing an answer to that prompt and look up for the next one.

After doing this several times, give students time to read through their thoughts and make any corrections they would like. Then they may upload their answers or share their thoughts with you or the class.

At this stage, you might correct any mistakes or emphasize the vocabulary shared. This is a great activity for generating ideas. It's even more fun if you participate too and take turns discussing your ideas with your student!

67. FREEWRITE

Freewriting is a technique in which students write continuously for a set period of time without regard to spelling, grammar, punctuation, or topic. Some writers use the technique to collect initial thoughts and ideas on a topic, often as a preliminary draft to more formal writing. A freewrite means that students are "free" to write whatever they want, but often it helps guide the freewrite with a prompt.

- Write about your favorite teacher.
- Write a letter to your future self.
- Write about your dream vacation.
- Write about your goals.
- Write about a friend you admire.
- Write about your family.
- Write about an important event you've had in your life.
- Write about your hobbies.
- Write about your biggest fears.
- Write about what you would do if you won a million dollars.
- Write a letter to your husband/wife/child/friend.
- Write about the qualities you admire most in someone.
- Write about your first love.

68. FAST-WRITES

A fast-write is similar to a freewrite because spelling, grammar, and vocabulary are not evaluated. However, what is evaluated is the number of words written in a given time. Students can gain a sense of accomplishment as they see their writing speed increase as they repeat the exercise. They are generally given an easy topic to fast-write about, and sometimes you will discuss the prompt ahead of time and elicit vocabulary words on the board before learners begin. For a fast-write to be accurate, you must ensure that the activity is done the same way every time.

Having students keep a writer's notebook where they can do their fast writing is a great way for them to keep track of their progress. They can literally see the proof of improvement on the pages. However, these fast-writes could also be done on the computer (which would make uploading to you easier). The problem is that some students are not as adept at typing as others, so then it becomes more a gauge of their typing skills and not their writing skills. It will be up to you to determine the best way for your students to complete these fast-write activities.

69. BRAINSTORMING

Brainstorming is an informal way of generating topics to write about. It's a wonderful way to start the writing process, both online or in the flipped classroom. Writers can brainstorm the topics for a whole paper or even for just a conclusion or an example. The important point about brainstorming is that there should be no pressure to be "brilliant." Students should simply open their minds to whatever pops into them. Think of it as a kind of free association.

For example, with an advanced group discussing poverty and education, you might say something like, "When I say 'literacy,' what pops into your mind?"

Much of what the students will come up with may not be useful, but that's okay. Part of brainstorming will involve a selection process. You might write students' ideas on the board, or invite a student to write down the ideas. You can also rephrase questions or add to questions to help students respond more fully. For example, you might ask, "Is literacy important? Why? or What do you think is blocking literacy today?"

Afterwards, you might go back to the question: "What else pops into your mind when I say literacy?" As a general rule, when brainstorming with a classroom, expect silence and expect the need for you to follow up with questions. You may also need to call on individuals, or invite students to speak in pairs and groups before sharing in front of the class.

70. VENN DIAGRAMS

A simple Venn diagram looks like two circles intersecting, and is often used as a pre-writing or post-writing activity. Venn diagrams are used to compare and contrast two subjects, objects, people, and so forth. Online teachers can use Venn diagram creators such as this popular generator found here:

http://www.readwritethink.org/files/resources/interactives/venn_diagrams/.

If you wanted learners to compare dolphins to sharks, you would ask students to place the similar items inside the parts of the circles that intersect (*fins, swim, eat fish*), and put items that are unique to dolphins (*mammals, play with humans*) and sharks (*sharp teeth, dangerous*) in each non-intersecting area.

This is a different type of brainstorming activity. Once students get all of their ideas placed into the diagram, they can begin writing. Students can choose to write about just one of the animals, or to compare and contrast both animals. It gives them a starting point when they might otherwise be stuck.

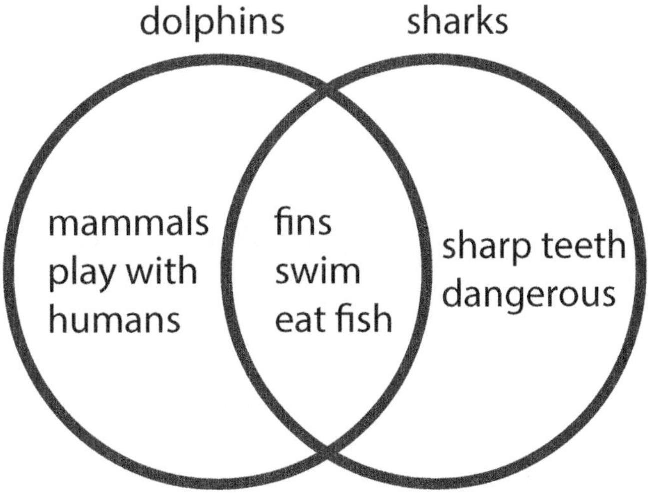

71. UNFINISHED STORIES

Ask students to finish a story or article. This can help them to predict the actual ending, and can also serve to have them imitate the tone and vocabulary of the reading. This activity can be done in groups or individually. In online formats, it is easiest to pair students together so that they can meet via videoconference, or to have them complete the assignment individually.

For advanced students, you could invite them to imitate the tone and vocabulary of the author, reminding them that each person's style of writing is a little different. Ask them to pay attention to the word choices, stylistic choices, and the voice and tone of the writing. If they are reading a magazine article, that will sound different than an essay. If they are reading a contemporary short story, that will sound different than a folktale. Have students pay attention to HOW the document is written, and then try to match the writing style.

72. ANY FOUR PICTURES MAKE A STORY

This activity requires students to think creatively and make connections. It can also be a lot of fun to see how students' imaginations differ. To do this activity, place any four random pictures on a wall, on a handout, or projected on the screen. If placing the pictures on the wall, make sure that they are printed large enough for all the students to see.

Then have students try to make a story based on those four pictures. Since the pictures are unrelated, the stories the learners generate are usually quite creative. You may want to help learners before they begin doing this activity by writing down vocabulary words that they do not know (invite them to ask questions about each picture to generate this list). Other requirements, such as the length of the story and any grammatical elements you wish to be included, should be specified.

Teachers often create this activity in Google slides.

73. GUESSWORK DICTATION (IMPOSSIBLE WORD CHALLENGE)

Here you will ask students to write down a few sentences that have been created, as in a normal dictation (see Top Ten Most Common Activities). In this activity, however, replace key vocabulary words with "impossibly big words"—that is, long, complex words that you think learners will not know.

Have students write out the dictation. For the big words, tell the students that it is okay to guess the spelling.

1. <u>Macroseisms</u> happen in Arizona all the time. (*earthquakes*)
2. Perhaps not a <u>superabundant</u> number like California, but quite a few. (*many*)
3. Flagstaff had the <u>inauspicious</u> honor of three major quakes early in the 20th century. (*unlucky*)

Read the sentences out loud just like in a normal dictation, and allow each student to write down what he or she hears. After, invite students to guess the meaning of the "impossible" word. Students often can remember key vocabulary better when they see a similar, more difficult word, and often enjoy the sound and complexity of larger words. It's a great way to practice figuring out words from context as well—an important reading skill.

74. REMEMBER THE PICTURE

Bring a picture that would be interesting for students to look at (you can find images online, or cut something from a magazine or advertisement). Consider a picture with a lot of detail, such as a picture with a lot of people on the beach, at a park, or in a mall doing different activities. Handouts can be shared with students before class via email or in a pre class video, or can be shared on the screen using Google slides or some other software.

Have students study the picture for one minute. Then remove the picture from their sight and have them write as much as they can remember. Students should be encouraged to focus on verbs or nouns, colors or shapes, or whatever language focus is being studied at the time.

As a variation, instead of having students write what they remember, ask them recall questions, such as What time of year was it? *Were there more people going up or down the escalator? Could you see any words?* Then show the image again to check answers.

75. DRAW YOUR NEIGHBORHOOD

Have students draw their own neighborhoods. Then have them share stories about their neighborhoods. They might want to discuss a time when they had a fight, their first crush, or other interesting stories. Students could draw online or upload a photo or scan of a picture they drew offline.

It is always helpful to share examples with students before beginning an activity like this. Before class, prepare a drawing of your own neighborhood, and during class point out specific places in your neighborhood where different stories happened to you. Tell them your stories with animation and excitement, and watch as they become excited to share their stories with you. You could even have a written version of your favorite story that you share with them to use as an example so they can see how it goes from drawing/brainstorming to telling to writing.

As an alternative to drawing their neighborhood, students could just draw their house, their bedroom, or a special place they have fond memories of (park, school, mountains, etc.). Then have them write stories about those places.

This is also a GREAT speaking activity, because students love to tell their stories. After they write, they can practice reading or telling their stories to the class.

76. POETRY WRITING

Often students are intrigued by different forms of poetry. You can use haiku, limericks, sonnets, and other forms to create engaging writing assignments.

One way to inspire learners to write in a language is to ask them to produce poetry using poetry templates. A poetry template can help a learner with various kinds of language tasks, and can help to motivate learners to share their lives and opinions. For example, notice this poetry template about "My Hero" that a student could follow to share some information about someone they think of as a hero.

MY HERO
Name:
Adjective, Adjective, Adjective:
Noun phrases **(HINT: WHAT IS HE/SHE?)**
Gerunds:
Prepositional Phrases:

MY HERO
Craig
Calm, Persuasive, Thoughtful
A wise soul, a steadfast rock, a gentle hand
Hearing, Changing, Becoming
Through all of his life.

Asking students to write and then post their poetry online can be very motivating, and a great way to lead students to appreciate the beauty of the language they are learning.

Part VII: Speaking Activities

Let him speak who has seen with his eyes.
– Congolese Proverb

Speaking activities have widely been seen as the most demanding for learners. This may be because of the many characteristics unique to spoken language: reduced forms, contractions, vowel reduction, and the use of slang. And let's not forget stress, rhythm, the use of signpost transitions, and so forth.

Speaking activities are also difficult for teachers. In part, this is because even short 5-minute speeches require a significant allocation of time to assess and provide feedback. Truly, how does one observe a student speaking for five minutes without boring the other twenty-nine students who are just waiting to give their presentations? Luckily, in the online classroom, many times you are working one on one with a student or with a smaller group of students, and you have the time necessary to really help them improve their speech.

Furthermore, speaking is difficult to assess since you are generally required to create rubrics that contain only some of the many possible categories that speaking entails. You must decide: Does speaking include the use of body language? Does speaking include the use of visual aids? These and similar questions demonstrate the difficulty of assigning precisely what speaking, and especially competent speaking, might be.

One simple solution is to simply provide a lot of informal, unassessed speaking practice in preparation for a few more formal events. Thus, many teachers try to get students talking as much as possible, without a focus on formal presentation but rather a focus on generating ideas, conversing, and practicing certain aspects of speaking.

The activities in this section mostly address this kind of informal speaking: speaking that may not be easily assessed but that allows students to engage in free, open communication practice. However, please pay special attention to the need to create narrow, specific objectives in these activities, and keep in mind that these informal practices should lead to success in a more formal evaluated presentation or speaking performance. Speaking activities, in this sense, take on the very real likeness of practice scrimmages before a big game.

77. WOULD YOU RATHER?

The game "Would You Rather" has been around for ages. You present students with two options that are equally unappealing, and they must choose what they would rather do/eat/see/experience. The difference here is that they must explain why they made their choice. This is often difficult for students to do because they don't want to make either choice ("Would you rather eat a live snake, or lay in a bathtub full of spiders? Why would you make that choice?").

Clearly you don't have to just choose options that are unappealing. You could present your students with options that are simply different, such as: "Would you rather be a land animal or a sea animal? Why?" or "Would you rather be super strong or super fast? Why?"
You can create Would you Rather questions based on a reading you did where the characters had to make a difficult choice, and you ask your students what they would have done in that situation. You can also ask Would you Rather questions based on video clips, static pictures, or listening prompts.

78. SENTENCE STARTERS

Sometimes students just need a little help getting started. Giving them simple prompts will help with this. You begin a sentence, and have the student finish it. This activity is similar to #65, for writing, but in this case, students speak the rest of the sentence. They can choose to just complete the prompt, or also continue and give a few follow-up sentences as well.

For example:

- I had so much fun with my friend when...
- Today at school, ...

- I wish I could have...
- The worst thing about today was...
- The best thing about today was...
- _____ makes me so mad because _____
- The reason I love _______ is ________
- I don't understand why _____
- If I could travel anywhere, it would be to _____ because _____

Try to use sentences that are open ended and leave room for more than a one-word answer. You can also choose prompts that would require or at least leave room for grammatical structures you have been practicing.

Sentences that connect with students and their lives work best, and then you can extend from the answers they give by asking them clarifying questions.

79. PICTURE PROMPT

Ask students to look at a picture and then talk to a partner about what they see. Choose pictures that help students respond to themes or vocabulary that they will need for more formal presentations. You may wish to provide a list of questions for students to respond to while looking at the picture. For example, if you are discussing climate change in class, you could show pictures that help students reflect on polar ice, rising sea levels, and animal habitats.

If you are teaching a lower level class, you can use a picture prompt with sentence frames that students can complete. Perhaps you have a picture of a man on the side of the road standing over the engine of a car while talking on his cell phone. You can ask questions like:

- What do you see in this picture?
- What problem does this man have?
- Who do you think he is calling on the phone?

Then provide them with sentence frames to answer the questions:

- I see ___________.
- The man's _______ is broken.
- I think he is calling _________.

80. THIS MAKES ME THINK THAT...

Students work in groups or pairs for this activity. The activity begins by you showing them an article or video. Afterwards, students should begin a discussion by saying, "This makes me think that..." Inform students that each member of the group should be allowed time to think and respond.

After everyone has responded to the material, invite students to respond to each other by using the phrase, "What you said makes me think that..." Tell students that they must continue speaking until you call the time or a timer goes off (you can decide beforehand how much time to allow for this).

This activity allows students to practice continued speech, and to practice listening as well, since they have to connect what they say to what they just heard.

81. AGREE/DISAGREE VALUE LINES pg. 76

Ask students a series of questions that they can agree or disagree with. After students agree and disagree, instruct them to rank the questions according to how much they agree/disagree with each statement, using the Value Lines template. Invite students to discuss why they ranked the value lines in that particular order. As a variation, instead of asking students to agree or disagree, you could ask them to love/hate, like/dislike, never done before/done before, or other kinds of classification.

To make more of a game out of this, you can play "Never Have I Ever," where students each hold up five fingers. One person makes a statement about something they have never done ("Never have I ever traveled to South America"). Any student who has traveled to South America would put one finger down. Each student takes turns, but is "out" when all their fingers are down. The person with any fingers remaining up at the end is the winner. This can then elicit conversation about some of the things people have or have not done, as well as what they would like to do, where they would like to go, and who or what they might like to see.

82. STORY CHAIN

If you're working with an online group, ask one student to begin a story. After a period of time (for example, one minute), the next person in the group must continue the story. This is done until the story has reached its conclusion or until every member has participated.

You can begin the story with a prompt that interests students or introduces the theme of your lesson. Tell students that it is fun to leave their section of the story at a moment of suspense. For example: "There was a man who was staring at a bag of chips. He hated these chips. He hated them a lot. This was because..."

This activity requires active listening as well as speaking, and gets students to pay attention to what is happening in the story. If a student is stuck, you can have word cards prepared where you give them a word and they then try to use that word in their story. This helps to give them ideas and get them thinking. For example:

> **Student 1**: One day I was at the beach. I decided to go surfing. As I was swimming out to the waves I saw...

Student 2: ...a shark! I was so scared, I didn't know what to do. I decided to...

Student 3: (*Student is stuck and can't think of anything, so you pull out one of your word cards and have them use it. The word is: whistle*). I decided to use my whistle to scare the shark and warn the other swimmers. The lifeguards heard my whistle and...

83. FOLKTALE STORYTELLING

Ask students to read a folktale and then recite it, by memory, to the rest of the group. If you have four stories of equal length, you can form groups and have each member read their story outside of class and share it with the rest of the group.

Because folktales are often written with a moral or lesson to be learned, have students discuss the lesson learned after retelling the story.

Ask students if there are any folktales from their country that are similar to the folktales they read. If so, what are the similarities and differences? (As an example, there are different versions of "Cinderella" and "Little Red Riding Hood" from different countries and cultures, but the lesson is basically the same.)

Another option is to have students each read a different version of the same folktale and then discuss the similarities and differences.

84. DISCUSSION QUESTIONS

While asking questions is a hallmark of every good teacher, it is a very commonly ignored aspect of teacher training. Asking questions to create discussions is an art and a vital skill. Consider the following tips for creating effective discussion questions:

- Ask questions that are open ended, NOT yes/no.
- Ask questions that are "come on" questions; in other words, that are dual-sided but elicit an emotional reaction because you have deliberately made it look one-sided (*Technology is bad, isn't it?*).
- Ask questions that make students think critically by asking them how they would resolve or respond to a particular problem.
- Ask questions and then give students time to think before the respond.
- Ask questions to specific students ahead of time and let them know you will be giving them time in class to answer.

85. CONVERSATION CARDS

Create conversation cards to have on hand. You can use these as a warm up, as a speaking activity, or as a time filler if you finish your lesson early and need something to do that is still educational and valuable.

Conversation cards are simply cards with questions on them that stimulate a conversation.

Some topics could include: family, holidays, "If you could", friends, hobbies, talents or skills they have, questions about their country or traditions, etc. The possibilities are endless. You

just want to be sure your questions are open ended, interesting, and that they will cause students to think and be able to practice their speaking skills. Some examples of good conversation card questions:

- Does your family have any special holiday traditions? Tell me about them.
- Do you eat special foods or go to a special place for different holidays?
- Tell me about a time when you were very scared. What happened?
- If you could have a super power, what would you choose and why?
- Who is someone you admire? What do you admire about this person?
- Can you recommend an interesting place to visit near your house?

Cards can be color-coded based on category, and you could have students pick a color, spin a spinner (there are online spinners available to use), or choose a number that correlates to a color, then ask questions from that category. You could also keep on hand a jar or hat filled with topics that you replenish regularly, and draw a topic when you need one.

As with all speaking, it is important to elicit conversation by asking questions, then clarifying with further questions. Even more fun is to have students ask you questions in return.

86. THREE THINGS IN A BACKPACK

Place three items in a backpack and explain to students that each of these three things has personal meaning (for example: a trophy, a picture, a ticket stub). Ask students to bring three objects of theirs to class or their next online session and share what the objects mean to them. The objects should be personal and interesting. The other students in the class should predict what each item might mean before the student shares.

As an alternative, you can describe something you have hidden in a backpack and have students try to guess what the object is before you show it. After they guess the object, have them ask you questions about the object and why it is special to you. This will elicit thinking, questioning, and speaking skills.

Part IX: Vocabulary Activities

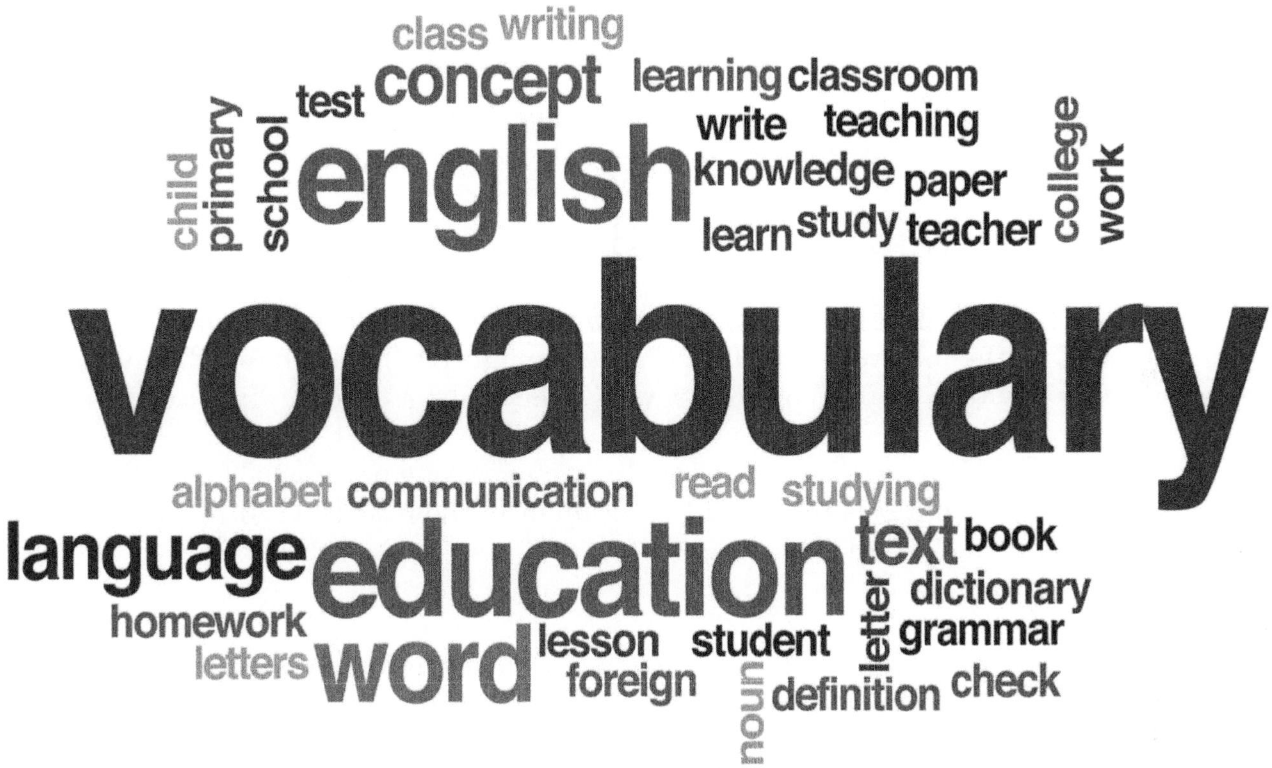

"Vocabulary enables us to interpret and to express. If you have a limited vocabulary, you will also have a limited vision and a limited future."
– Jim Rohn

Vocabulary is often a favorite for language teachers. This is likely because it is easy to give learners a list, and it is easy to provide definitions and give tests. One of the problems, however, is that much of the time vocabulary learning is not durable. This means that students are likely to forget the vocabulary shortly after a period of intense study and test taking. Thus, the best vocabulary activities should help students remember and practice a vocabulary word more than once, and in multiple contexts.

The activities in this section are intended to do just this: help learners use and practice key vocabulary. A number of theorists would agree with the idea that vocabulary must be seen and used multiple times (some say at least seven times!) in order to be remembered and used. Make sure, as a teacher, that you don't commit the unpardonable language sin of teaching a vocabulary word once, and then expecting students to remember and use it.

87. I SPY

This activity is a variation on the popular children's game. Choose a vocabulary word and then pick a specific characteristic of the word. For example, you might say, "I spy with my little eye a word that is a noun. It is used in eating." (referring to *fork*). The students then try to guess the word. Additional hints can be provided as needed. (If necessary, explain to students that they won't actually "see" the item anywhere, but only need to see it in their mind's eye.)

This activity can be done synchronously or asynchronously as needed. For asynchronous settings, post the first prompt on your social media page or in a discussion forum and let students comment on it. You can provide additional hints in the comments as well.

88. SPACED REPETITION (THE LEITNER SYSTEM)

Instruct learners to make flashcards and to review these flashcards at intervals or spaces. Tell them to think of the intervals like "boxes" (see the figure below). They will have one box they review every day (box 1), one box they review every 2 days (box 2), and so on.

Tell students that if they answer a card correctly, it moves "one box down" (meaning from 2 to 3, or 3 to 4) so that it is reviewed less frequently the next time. If it is answered incorrectly, it moves "one box up" (meaning from 4 to 3, or 3 to 2) so that it is reviewed more frequently in the future.

As students practice and review the cards, they will all eventually move to the least frequently reviewed box and only need to be reviewed perhaps once a month. As more cards move up, students can add more cards to the lower boxes and begin the cycle again.

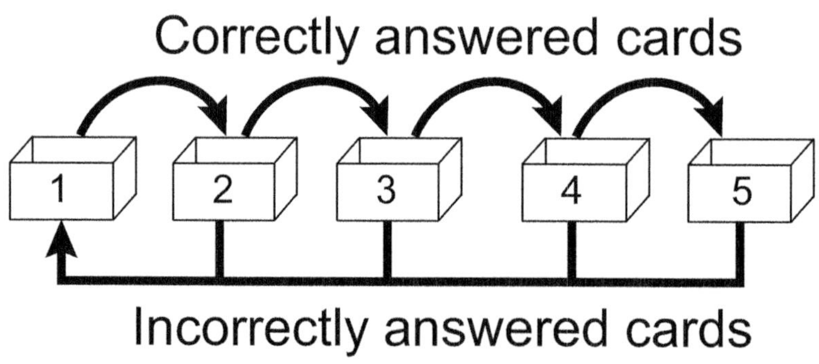

There are several technology solutions currently available that let students create digital flashcards. One of the most popular ones at the time of this writing is Quizlet (www.quizlet.com). Students can create a free account and start creating their own cards almost immediately. If you pay for a teacher account, you can create classes and monitor how often students practice flashcard sets you have created. Quizlet does not have spaced repetition built in as a feature, but students can easily move cards from one set to another, so they could use sets of cards as their "boxes" and have one set they review every day, one set they review every two days, and so forth.

Another popular online solution is http://brainscape.com. Brainscape does have spaced repetition built in, and like Quizlet, it is free to create flashcards. If you want to track students' progress, you will need to pay for a pro account. Another solution is the Anki app, which includes spaced repetition and works on most mobile devices. Anki is available for free at the time of this writing.

89. REBUS

A rebus strip replaces words with clip art, giving students a chance to practice vocabulary by reading aloud the word every time they see the image.

For example, instead of the word *chicken*, replace the word with a small image of a chicken  and ask students to say aloud the word when they encounter the image.

A rebus strip can be read in pairs or as a group with you. Students can also practice reading them to family members, friends, or anyone in their ecosystem. Or, they can record themselves reading it in a video and upload it to the course platform.

Another great activity is to have students create their own rebus strips and share them with their classmates. You might want to have a rebus strip competition, where students vote for the ones they like most.

90. MIX AND MATCH (ALSO COMMONLY CALLED CONCENTRATION)

Mix and Match involves having a number of words written on cards, with picture or definition cards that correspond. For example, if the word on the card is *skyscraper*, you should have another card with a picture or definition of the word skyscraper. It is usually best to have no more than 20 matching pairs. (For online teaching, there are ways to create these cards digitally and display them on the screen instead of as physical cards.)

The words and pictures are randomly placed in their own groups, face side down, on a board or on the ground. Invite a learner to turn over only two cards, one from each group. Learners remove a single picture or word from one group and try to match it with its counterpart, in the other but if the learner chooses two pictures that do not correspond, they must be turned back over in the precise location. The student can keep pairs that are successfully matched, and the student or team with the most matching pairs wins the game.

As with digital flashcards, there are many technology solutions for playing Mix and Match. Some digital flashcard solutions include this as a way of reviewing cards. Others let you create the game and then share it with your students so they can play it online. You could also have students create the game using physical cards, and then play it on their own or with people in their language ecosystem.

91. COLLOCATIONAL RELATIONSHIPS

Collocational Relationships is a game that requires students to find the natural relationships that exist among words. For example, the words bear and honey could appear on a sheet. The students would be required to draw two arrows between bear and honey. The students then have to consider the relationship from bear to honey (with the arrow pointing from *bear* to *honey*) and also the relationship from honey to bear (with the arrow pointing from honey to bear). Then students should use words/sentences that make the relationship clear.

Sentences from Bear to Honey:

> *Bears like honey. Bears are happy when they eat honey. Bears eat honey.*

Sentences from Honey to Bear:

> *Honey pleases bears. Honey gives bears smiles. Honey is a treasure for bears.*

The relationships need to be grammatically correct and should demonstrate an understanding of the connectedness of the words, and can also be an easy way to introduce collocations.

If you include several words on the page, students can find their own relationships, which can lead to some interesting discussions and sentences. Students can share their sentences via a discussion forum and have fun creating sentences from the collocational relationships posted by other students.

92. JAZZ CHANTS

Jazz chants are repetitive mnemonic devices that help students recall information through rhyme and rhythm. There are hundreds of jazz chants to choose from online, or you can invent your own. If you are teaching in a synchronous setting, you can invite learners to clap out the rhythm and repeat the chant with you. Or you could record yourself performing the chant and have students follow along on their own.

A fun extension activity might be to have students create their own jazz chants and then either perform them in front of the class, or record themselves performing their jazz chant and share the video with the class.

> *Say, said.*
> Stop on red.
> *Eat, ate.*
> Don't be late.
> *Break, broke.*
> Have a Coke.
> *Take, took.*

Learn to cook.
Speak, spoke.
Tell a joke.
Write, wrote.
Get off the boat.

93. TWENTY QUESTIONS OR TWENTY HINTS

Tell students that you will ask them to guess which word from a list of vocabulary words you are thinking about. For Twenty Questions, tell them they will get to ask 20 yes/no questions about your word. Possible questions might include "Is it a noun?" or "Does it start with the letter J?"

You may choose to limit the type of questions students can ask to prevent guessing based on non-linguistic features of the word. If you have only one word that starts with "J" on your list, for example, you may want to restrict them from asking questions about the spelling of the word. Remind students that you can only answer "yes" or "no" to their questions and cannot provide any additional information as part of your answers. If the students guess the word before they ask all of their 20 questions, they win, and you can start again. You can ask the student who guessed the word to lead the next round.

For Twenty Hints, start by beginning with the phrase "I am a word that…" in order to create more interest. Tell the students that you will give them 20 hints, one at a time, and after each hint, they will have one chance to guess the word. If they get the word right before they use all 20 hints, they win.

If you are teaching in an asynchronous setting, you can set this activity up using a discussion forum. You can provide one hint at a time, and students can submit their guesses. With some discussion forums, you can require students to post before they can read other students' posts, which can prevent them from guessing based on what other students have posted.

94. THE WORD TRAIN

This activity works great for practicing Latin roots, prefixes and suffixes. Start with a word that contains two morphemes, such as "conduct" (*con*, meaning together; *duc*t meaning to lead). Then connect another two-part word that uses a root, prefix, or suffix from the first word, such as "composition" (*com*, meaning together; *pos*, meaning to place or put). Add a third word that uses the newly added word part, such as "deposit", and a fourth word, such as "decelerate", and so on.

You could post the first word in a discussion forum, and then challenge your students to see how many connections they can make. You could also provide students with the first word and the last word and see if they can fill in the connecting words.

95. SENTENCE STARTERS: WHAT'S MY LINE

Give students a handout with several "sentence starters" on it. A sentence starter is the beginning of a sentence such as *I will always remember...* or *Sometimes I wish....*

Tell students that you will begin, and choose one of the sentence starters and finish it. For example, *I love to ... give successful students an A in this class.* Then choose a student and a sentence starter for them: "Juan, what will you never forget?" Juan says something like, "I will never forget...the time I lost my passport". When Juan is done, he chooses another student and a sentence starter for them in the same manner, and you continue until all the students have completed a sentence using a sentence starter from the sheet.

As a teacher, you will need to help students to prompt the next student by creating a question from each prompt. At more basic levels, it might work better to invite students to choose their own prompt instead of having the previous student choose it for them. That way they can choose a prompt they are more familiar with. If you run out of prompts, you can have students re-use them, creating different sentences each time. At advanced levels, it might work well to have students do this exercise in pairs or groups, and allow follow-up sentences or small discussions that naturally arise.

This is a fun activity to do on social media with students, where they post their sentence and the name of the next student, who then posts as a comment in the thread.

Part X: Teaching Language Learner Autonomy

"Self-education is, I firmly believe, the only kind of education there is."
– Isaac Asimov

Online learning faces a number of challenges, perhaps chief of which is the fact that it involves so many self-directed techniques. Learners must be aware of deadlines, look for resources, and as soon as they click away from you as a teacher, now find themselves alone to complete assignments. Without a teacher as both resource (*Teacher, I have a question!*) and parent (*Son, I was just looking over your shoulder and I noticed...*), it becomes all the more important for learners to not only value their independence but to learn how to navigate and embrace it.

You must recognize that they play a key role in the learner autonomy of the student. Provide necessary guidance that will empower students. This empowerment can and should happen in a number of ways.

1. Online students need reminding. Just like students in a brick and mortar classroom, you must be in constant contact with students. This can happen in a weekly announcement, for example. Announcements can remind students of key deadlines, give feedback that is specific to the entire group, and provide techniques and suggestions for difficult assignments. You might want to consider both video and written announcements. Video announcements add a visual component to an otherwise sterile environment, and written announcements can clearly delineate tasks in a way that is clear (many online teachers prefer bulleted and bolded texts).

2. Online students need modeling + reinforcement. Online students may be asked to do things they are not accustomed to... like recording a video of themselves. Providing models beforehand is extremely important so they know what is expected. Perhaps even more important is that they need to be encouraged and praised when they are able to do something new. Make sure to provide feedback, especially for those things that represent a new technique or skill that will prove useful throughout the online learning experience.

3. Online learners need a guide to build an ecosystem. Developing learner autonomy is not something easily achieved, and you must know not only how to develop knowledge of the language but how to develop students' ability to learn a language on their own... especially in an online environment. Teaching and motivating students to navigate the online world may mean that you must learn a language online yourself. As you do, you may discover hidden resources and strategies yourself that encourage your own students' growth.

All in all, your focus on learner autonomy will mean that you are not only a teacher within an online classroom setting but that you have a clear understanding of what it means to develop a language ecosystem for your learners. In order to help you help your students develop language learner autonomy, we present a few useful activities that will boost your ability to develop a learner ecosystem and give you some ideas of just what language learner autonomy is all about.

96. INDIVIDUAL LANGUAGE PLANS

Creating an individual language plan can help you guide learners to realize that they play a part in their own language learning success. Many online teachers use an individual language plan (ILP) with their learners at the beginning of a course, which then serves as both a get-to-know-you form and an action plan. Creating the ILP with a learner allows the learner to create goals, locate resources, and think about language learning in a self-directed way. Access and even download a sample plan here: https://language-warriors.com/ilp.pdf

An individual language plan asks students to identify four key sources for using and practicing language outside the online classroom.

1. **Goals:** Learners are invited to set a short-term and long-term goal. You can help to guide learners to set goals that are both achievable and ambitious. This can also help you understand a learner's particular ambitions and needs.

2. **Internet Resources:** Learners write down the language learning resources they are already familiar with. This might be language learning apps, dictionaries, or online tools for translation or language practice. You might choose to add to that list or give suggestions that they may not have heard about. This exchange of information can provide valuable feedback to you about what technologies your learners are interested in, and what technologies you might want to introduce.
3. **Friends**: Ask learners to write down who they know who might serve as a language partner. While it might be members of the class, it is important to ask them to extend their language learning to those who might already speak the language in their home and community. There is considerable research that demonstrates that successful students are those who use local resources (the closer the better) to improve their language abilities.
4. **Tools:** Another aspect to a language plan is to invite learners to find and use resources in the form of tools. By tools, what is meant is a language strategy or technique such as prediction, think alouds, predict-prepare-perform, and others that successful language learners tend to use. Since most learners fail at learning a language because of the improper use of technique, learning successful strategies is key. A brief overview of strategies can be found in the online course Learning How to Learn a Language. Another resource is the book, The Language Learner Guidebook, which helps learners to build entire language ecosystems for themselves and others. Finally, The Language Map is a useful tool to help learners complete four strategies a month and can be used by you to assign tasks outside of the classroom in an organized and motivational way.

Learning How to Learn a Language
https://www.udemy.com/course/learning-how-to-learn-a-language/

The Language Learner Guidebook
https://language-warriors.com/language-guidebook

The Language Map
https://language-warriors.com/language-map

97. CHALLENGES

Learners who engage in language exposure outside of the classroom are likely to learn faster and better than those who do not. Assigning such reading through challenges and reading logs is an excellent way to promote language literacy and the love of language in general.

A challenge is a weekly goal that students assign to themselves. You invite a learner or group of learners to decide what might be a difficult number of pages to read (for some classes, it might be five pages, for others, it might be fifty). Such a challenge might create an incentive for students who complete the assignment.

Challenge: We will read 15 pages this week.
Incentive: Students who complete this goal will be put on the wall of fame.

Challenge: We will read 25 pages this week.
Incentive: If all students complete this challenge, I will sing a silly song.

Challenge: We will read 50 pages this week.
Incentive: Those who finish will receive my favorite story sent to them in a PDF.

Challenge: We will read 100 pages.
Incentive: The student who reads 100 pages will receive a special gift.

Incentives are sometimes negotiated, but might involve even more opportunities for learning success or some sort of exciting motivational technique.

Challenges are best used with reading, vocabulary, and listening logs.

98. READING, VOCABULARY, AND LISTENING LOGS

pgs. 81&82

A log allows students to record each day or week the amount and type of material they are consuming. Learners often like to share, for example, a book they are reading, a show they are watching, or words that they are learning.

While logs do not have to be a formal part of the class, they can form an essential part of a learner's experience. In other words, you don't generally assess what a learner reads or watches in a log, you mostly encourage it as a part of the students' overall learning experience.

Reading Logs

A reading log allows students to show what they are reading outside of your online class. There should be a set time each week when students are able to share with each other or you about what they read. They can write down answers to questions, discuss what they liked about what they read, ask questions to others who have read the same book, or whatever you would like to have them do in the reading log.

A reading log simply means that you invite students to engage in what they are reading. One reading teacher used a reading log to help students use the vocabulary they learned in the reading. This teacher asked students to write sentences using the words they did not know prior to the reading. Another reading teacher invited students to write a story based on a minor character, or write as if they were one of the characters.

Listening/Vocabulary Logs

In a listening or vocabulary log, learners write down what material they are watching (movies, music, shows). As with reading logs, having a set time for learners to share what they watched and learned is key. By reviewing any newly learned vocabulary they have written down or questions about expressions they heard, a teacher can often have impromptu lessons about words that they are likely hearing at their correct level.

99. CONVERSATION CLUB/CONVERSATION PARTNER

Conversation Club

A conversation club is a place where students can gather outside of a classroom. In the online world, chatrooms are places where conversation clubs are often created by teachers to encourage students to participate in discussions. Some learning management systems may have their own chatroom options as well. Google Hangouts, Zoom, and Skype also have chatroom capabilities.

A chatroom is often improved when there is a conversation topic. You may wish students to speak about a classroom topic, or provide additional topics in a less structured fashion. You can also prepare a list of questions for students to answer, and discuss those questions using a discussion moderator.

The moderator could be you or a designated student. If the student serves as a moderator, you may want to train the moderator ahead of time on the pace of each question, the kinds of responses that are expected, and the need to allow and encourage each participant to speak.

Conversation clubs can be engaging and fun, and should not be as formal as other activities. Encouraging chatrooms beyond the classroom is a vital part of ecosystem training, so make sure you encourage students to make their own groups and form conversation clubs on their own.

Conversation Partners

Sometimes a group is too unwieldy or difficult to manage, especially if your online students come from different parts of the world and live in different time zones. Assigning students to meet in pairs online might help overcome this particular problem. Encourage students to meet regularly to discuss homework assignments, share ideas, and simply enjoy conversation in the target language. When possible, assigning students who do not speak the same native language is preferable.

100. LANGUAGE MISSIONS/LANGUAGE MAP

Language Missions

The most successful language learners tend to be ones that see language learning as a series of active tasks. An active task can mean many things, but we define it as a task in which learners take responsibility for their own learning, accomplish something within the language that is challenging, and create something that is satisfying to the learner.

Our motivational way of extending this idea of an active task is by rebranding it as a language mission. A language mission is an active task or assignment, but one that has the added component of being fun. Language missions allow learners to explore resources and share with friends. Language missions might include the following:

1. finding and sharing a favorite song
2. writing a poem to someone you admire (about why you admire him or her)
3. learning about a city you want to visit and writing about it to someone you want to invite to come with you
4. writing a thank you letter to a past language teacher
5. writing an elevator speech just in case you ever meet your favorite celebrity

You'll notice that each of these activities is motivational in that it is communicative at its core... and that learners will naturally want to share what they have created.

The Language Map

The language map teaches students how to go on language missions. Once completed, students will have completed 48 language missions. Feel free to watch the first video here to learn more.

Language Map Intro:
https://www.youtube.com/

The Language Map
https://language-warriors.com/language-map

Bonus Activity

101. SHOW AND TELL

The basic premise behind show-and-tell activities is that students are motivated to share ideas and objects that are valuable to them. This is no different in an online or flipped classroom design. Students of all ages can share an object that represents something of personal significance. Objects that are most interesting tend to be those that elicit a personal story or journey. For example, a learner might bring in a swim trophy and then explain what it meant to work for and achieve that trophy. A learner might bring in a family heirloom and explain the story behind the heirloom and why it has been kept in the family. Alternatively, an object can be used to demonstrate a particular skill, like a musical instrument or a favorite food. In this case, learners can share about the process (how to play the flute, how to make a tropical smoothie).

Show-and-tell activities can be rather wide open, although often giving a teacher model is useful. Students often like to learn about you in a more personal way, and you can demonstrate certain aspects of the show-and-tell through the modeling (length of the presentation, types of language forms used, etc.).

You might wish to have students share their own activity in both spoken and written form in order to further discuss the kinds of language/vocabulary that is used. You could also show exemplary student models from the past to give students an idea of possibilities and expectations.

Part XI: Templates/Activity Resource

This final section presents templates that should help you recognize the importance of engaging students through the use of graphic organizers.

Since you cannot hand out sheets of paper to students very easily in an online format, often you will have to create these types of organizers by sharing your screen with participants. You could also post or email a file and ask students to fill out a particular template or form.

When you want students to have physical copies of these organizers, you may need to give them some time to print out a particular template since some may not have access to a printer in their own homes.

For those of you who have the technological skills, you may wish to create templates that can be filled out electronically, such as PDF fillable worksheets or online worksheets.

Finally, for those of you that are teaching in a blended format, feel free to print as many copies of these worksheets as necessary.

Activity 2: Cloze Passage

"Scarborough Fair"

(English Folk Song)

Directions: This song is a traditional love song often sung by a man asking a woman to do impossible things, followed by a woman asking a man to do impossible things. As you listen, please fill in the words from the blanks. When the song is over, talk to a partner and answer the following questions: Why would people who love each other ask for the impossible?

(Man)

Are you going to Scarborough (1) ________________?
Parsley, sage, rosemary, and thyme.
Remember me to one who lives there.
She once was a true love of mine.
Tell her to make me a cambric (2) ________________.
Parsley, sage, rosemary, and thyme.
Without no seam nor (3) ________________.
Then she'll be a (4) ____________ love of mine.

(Woman)

Tell him to find me an acre of (5) __________.
Parsley, sage, rosemary, and thyme.
Between the salt water and the sea (6) ______________.
Then he'll be a true love of mine.
Are you going to Scarborough (1) _______?
Parsley, sage, rosemary, and thyme.
Remember me to one who lives there.
He once was a (4) _____________ love of mine.

Vocabulary answers

1. Fair
2. shirt
3. needlework
4. true
5. land
6. Stand

Activities 23, 24, and 81: Value Lines

Directions: Your teacher will give some statements. Mark how much you agree with each statement by marking an x on the line, or circle the face if you **completely** disagree or agree.

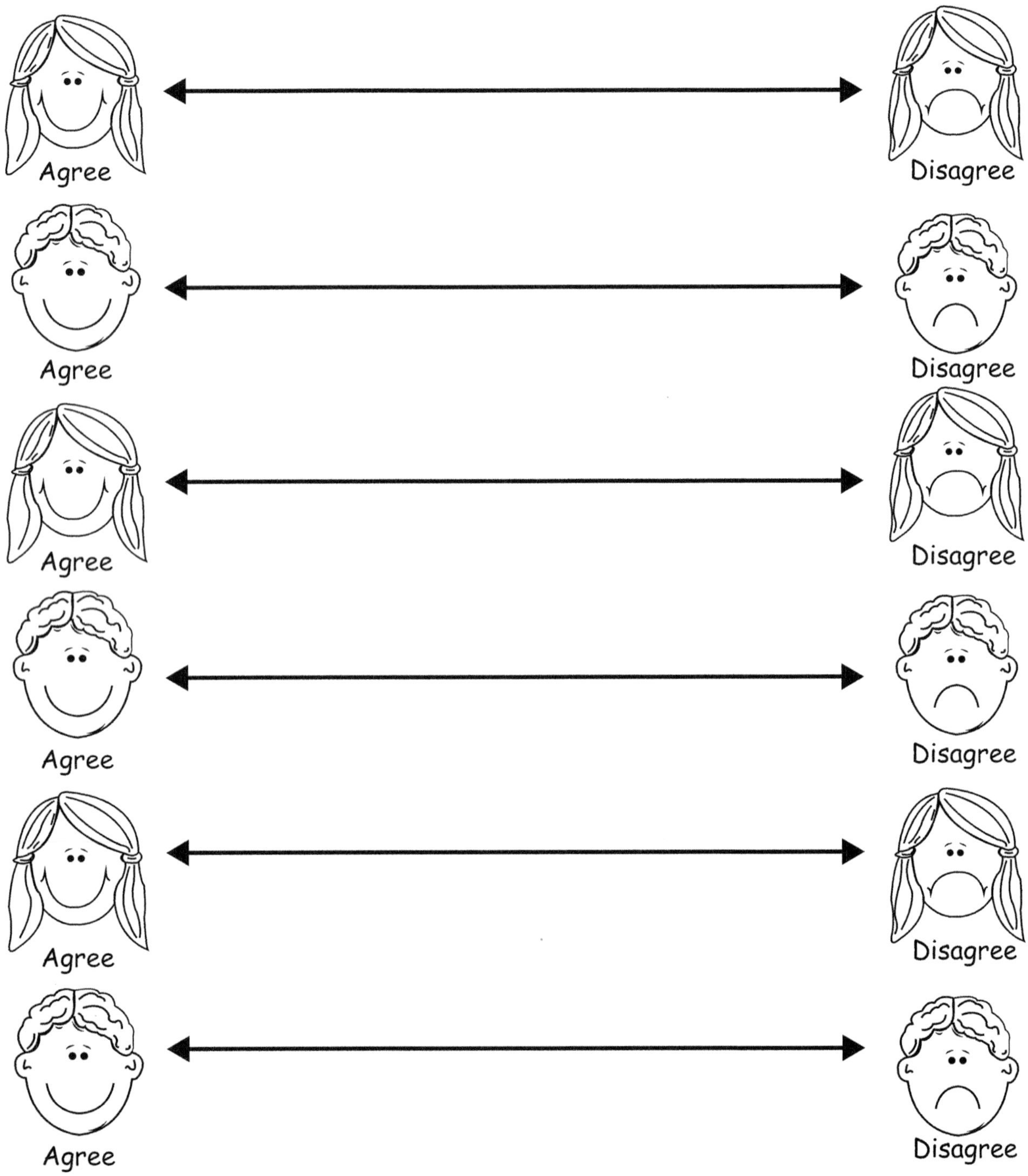

Activity 55: Reader's Outline

Directions: As you read, look for three or more main ideas. Under each main idea, what are the subtopics under each idea? And under the sub-topics, are there points and even more points the author makes? Use the following outline provided below to write an outline of the reading.

Heading:

1. Main Topic
    a. Sub Topic
        i. points under the subtopic
        ii. more points
        iii. even more points
    b. Sub Topic 2
        i. points under the subtopic
        ii. more points
        iii. even more points
2. Main Topic 2
    a. Sub Topic
        i. points under the subtopic
        ii. more points
        iii. even more points
    b. Sub Topic 2
        i. points under the subtopic
        ii. more points
        iii. even more points
3. Main Topic 3
    a. Sub Topic
        i. points under the subtopic
        ii. more points
        iii. even more points

Activity 56: Mapping

Directions: Choose a character. Find three characteristics that are worth exploring. Find examples to support each of the characteristics you have chosen.

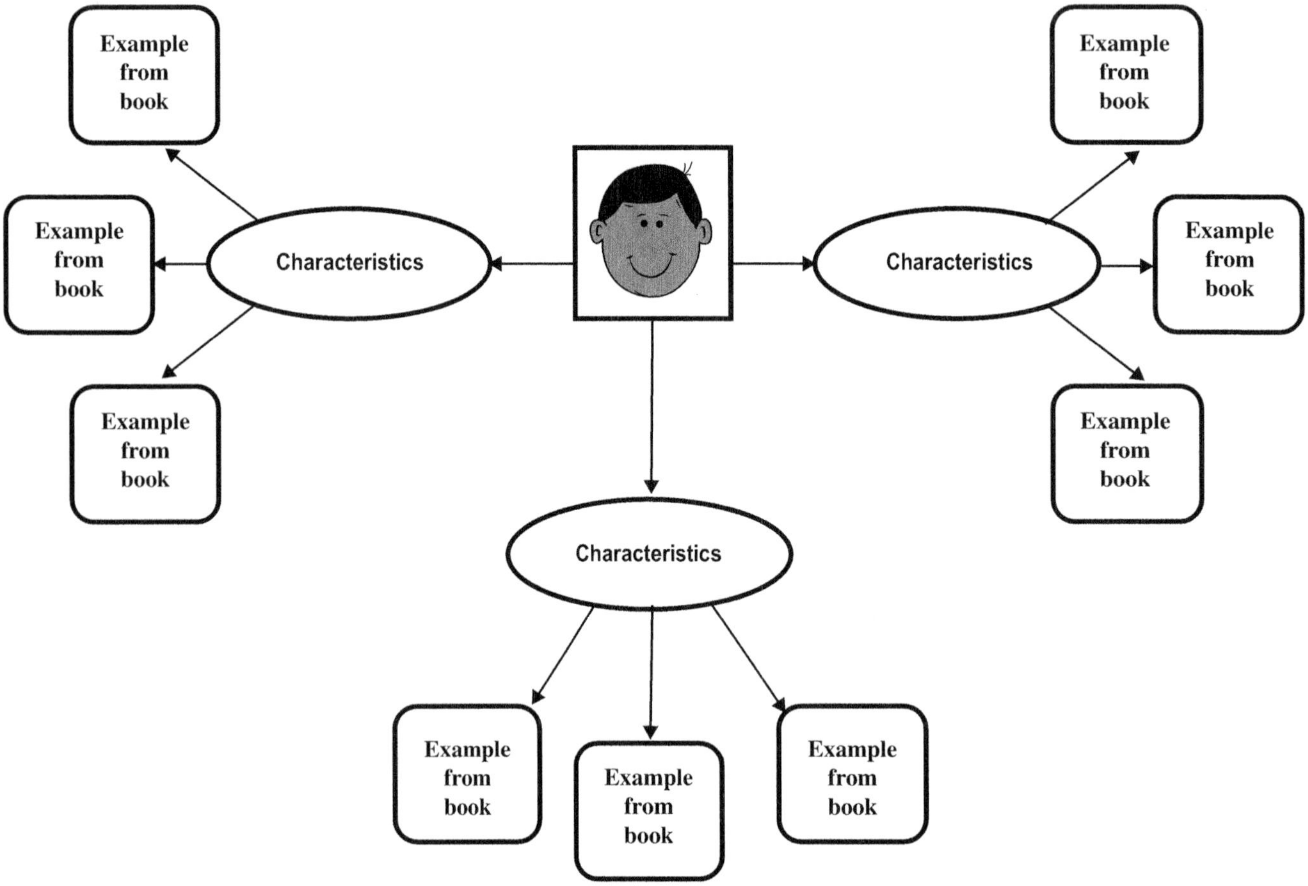

Activity 59: Reading Mapp

Directions for a Reading: After reading a story, think of the main idea, supporting details, and purpose of the story. Then write your own personal reaction to the story. (Example based on the story, "No Speak English" from the *House on Mango Street*, by Sandra Cisneros.)

Main Idea	**A**nalysis of Supporting Details
To show the difficulties of a working immigrant's wife and her barriers to learn English and fit in.	*1. Doesn't leave the house* *2. Complains to husband* *3. Sings songs from her country* *4. Looks at pictures* *5. Tries to stop boy from speaking English*
Purpose	**P**ersonal Reaction
To inform us to understand a situation, to make us feel compassion for Mamacita	*I liked this story a lot. It made me want to visit Mamacita and give her some advice.*

Main Idea	**A**nalysis of Supporting Details
Purpose	**P**ersonal Reaction

Activity 60: Rank Order Exercise

Directions: While you are reading, write down the ideas that seem most important to you. After you finish reading, decide which ideas are most importantor most interesting. Put the most important or interesting point first, then the second, third, fourth, and so on. Be prepared to discuss why you put these ideas in this order.

Ideas	Ranking (order of importance or interest)
	1
	2
	3
	4
	5
	6

Activity 98: Reading Log for________________________________

	Date	# of Pages Read	Name of Book/Article	Words/Idioms Learned
1				
2				
3				
4				
5				
6				
7				
8				
9				
10				
11				
12				
13				
14				
15				
16				
17				
18				
19				
20				
21				
22				
23				
24				
25				
Total				

Activity 98: Listening/Vocabulary Log for____________________

(A record of the words and phrases learned while you watch movies and shows)

	Word/Idiom	Definition		Word/Idiom	Definition
1			26		
2			27		
3			28		
4			29		
5			30		
6			31		
7			32		
8			33		
9			34		
10			35		
11			36		
12			37		
13			38		
14			39		
15			40		
16			41		
17			42		
18			43		
19			44		
20			45		
21			46		
22			47		
23			48		
24			49		
25			50		

About the Authors

Dr. Shane Dixon, Senior Global Educator, Arizona State University

Dr. Dixon has 20 years of TESOL experience, and has taught in Venezuela, Mexico, Iraq, and the US. He has helped design teacher training programs for groups from China, Korea, Japan, Iraq, Peru, and Mexico, and has created language programs for companies such as General Electric (Brazil), LG (Korea), and Toyota (Japan). He is the co-designer of the popular series, Teach English Now! at www.coursera.org, where he helps thousands of aspiring teachers obtain a TESOL Certificate from Arizona State University. He holds a doctorate in educational technology from Arizona State University and a master's in English (with an emphasis in language planning and policy) from Brigham Young University. He is the author of 100 TESOL Activities: Practical ESL/EFL Activities for the Communicative Classroom.

Dr. Justin Shewell, Language and Education Specialist, Arizona State University

Dr. Shewell is the co-designer and primary producer for the largest TESOL certificate course in the world, Teach English Now! This program, currently on the Coursera platform, boasts 250,000 learners from 194 different countries. He has taught English in the Middle East, Asia, and the United States. He is the author of 50 Ways to Teach Online, and several other book chapters and articles on language teaching and using technology in the language classroom. He is a regular presenter at international and regional conferences on language teaching and educational technology. Dr. Shewell holds a Ph.D. in Educational Technology from Arizona State University and a Master's degree in Teaching English to Speakers of Other Languages from Brigham Young University.

Jenny Crandell, Online English Teacher, adjunct reading faculty for Chandler Gilbert Community College, adjunct education faculty for Mary Lou Fulton Teachers College for Arizona State University

Jenny has 23 years of teaching experience, including elementary school, online, and at the collegiate level. She has a Master's degree in Elementary Education with a reading endorsement, as well as a TESOL certificate earned through Dr. Dixon's and Dr. Shewell's Teach English Now! course on Coursera. Jenny has taught English to Chinese students online for the past three years, and was privileged to teach English in Jinan, China. She helps recruit teachers and students to do an international exchange program in China each summer. Currently she teaches reading courses at a local community college, as well as courses at ASU for students in the Mary Lou Fulton Teacher Education program, and supervises students while in their student teaching residency.

Printed in Great Britain
by Amazon

41410014R00054